BOUND FOR PLAY

BDSM TRAINING MANUAL

Mistress Flame and Master Paul

BOUND FOR PLAY
BDSM TRAINING MANUAL

First published in Australia by Mistress Flame and Master Paul 2019

Copyright © Mistress Flame and Master Paul 2019
All Rights Reserved

 A catalogue record for this book is available from the National Library of Australia

ISBN: 978-0-6485881-0-8 (pbk)
ISBN: 978-0-6485881-1-5 (ebk)

Typesetting and design by Publicious Book Publishing
Published in collaboration with Publicious Book Publishing
www.publicious.com.au

No part of this book may be reproduced in any form, by photocopying or by any electronic or mechanical means, including information storage or retrieval systems, without permission in writing from both the copyright owner and the publisher of this book.

Disclaimer

This is an instruction manual for adults of consenting age, (which in Australia is eighteen years of age, though this will vary in other countries) and with the legal and mental capacity to make their own decisions and take responsibility for their actions. The presenters of this information accept no responsibility for the actions of the readers of this material. This manual is intended as a guide only, and individuals must assess their own circumstances before attempting any potentially dangerous role-play scenarios. Throughout this manual, the presenters continually advise the readers on aspects of health, safety and hygiene that need to be considered and addressed prior to any role-play session. It is acknowledged in some countries even though consent has been given, it is illegal to practice sexual activities that physically hurt another.

Contents

1. Introduction ... 1
2. Objectives of the Presenters ... 3
3. Where do you stand? ... 5
4. Entering the world of BDSM ... 7
5. How to start ... 13
6. Use of common household items ... 18
7. Definition of a BDSM relationship ... 24
8. Safe words and general safety ... 34
9. Hygiene ... 38
10. Consent ... 40
11. Limits ... 42
12. Checklist ... 44
13. Agreement ... 46
14. Clothing ... 48
15. Appearance ... 52
16. Body language ... 54
17. BDSM vs. abuse ... 56
18. Roles and names ... 59
19. Professional vs. private/casual BDSM activities ... 64
20. Physical vs. mental activities ... 66
21. Full-time sessions ... 69
22. Contacts ... 71
23. Equipment and maintenance ... 73
24. Courtesy ... 87
25. Etiquette ... 89
26. Acceptance of roles ... 90
27. Guide to roleplay ... 91
28. Specific activities ... 97
    - ✓ Tying a triple loop and cinch ... 97
    - ✓ Tying a rope body harness ... 99
    - ✓ Performing a hog tie ... 104

✓ Conducting a full spanking session	106
✓ Effective mummification	111
✓ Complete cross dressing	116
✓ Enforcing public humiliation	119
✓ Serving and other household chores	121
29. Example scenarios	**123**
✓ Starting a role-play session	123
✓ Public humiliation	126
✓ Public exhibitionism	127
✓ Bondage Parlour visit	128
✓ Dinner party scenario	144
Glossary of terms	**151**
Appendix A	
✓ Sample checklist	157
Appendix B	
✓ Sample slavery contract	173
About the Author	**181**

1

Introduction

Many people fantasise about a wild sex life. For some, kinky sex may be thrilling because it pushes their limits and for others it may be the voyeuristic aspect only. Here is an opportunity to open your mind to the exciting world of Bondage, Discipline, Sadism and Masochism (from here on referred to as BDSM). See chapter five for a full definition.

This manual will use the experiences of a couple, Mary and Fred and their step-by-step introduction into the BDSM world. It follows Mary's progression from a novice to confident 'Mistress' and Fred's dream of playing a 'sub'. (These are described as Dominant and submissive, from here on called 'Domme/Dom' and 'sub'). You too can follow the learning curve as Mary and Fred did and experience the pleasures they found in their new fantasy world.

This manual provides potential Mistresses, Masters and submissives with vital information so that by the time you read the conclusion, you should be capable of entering the BDSM world in your chosen role.

INTRODUCTION

Presenters

Mistress Flame:

Mistress Flame entered the BDSM world after teaming up with Master Paul. Following initial experiments and experiences as a sub to Master Paul, She has since assumed a Dominant role. Mistress Flame provided Her services for many years on a professional basis to clientele in Sydney.

Master Paul:

Master Paul entered the BDSM world as a sub, visiting various bondage parlours since the 1970's. He has experimented with scenarios both as a sub and Dom. Sadly, he passed away from illness in 2018 with his dream of this manual, yet to be realised.

2

Objectives of the Presenters

The objectives of the presenters are to introduce novices into the BDSM fantasy world as well as provide experienced players with fresh ideas. Whether the participants wish to take a Dominant or a submissive role, there are several vital aspects that need to be understood. The presenters will recommend these as they become pertinent to the topic under discussion.

The presenters only promote BDSM role-play that is s**afe, sane, and consensual.** At all times, the readers are encouraged to always regard s**afety, health and hygiene** as major considerations whenever they are participating in BDSM role-play scenarios.

Furthermore, the presenters have set their own standards of behaviour for involvement in the BDSM scene. Apart from the safety, health and hygiene aspects, these standards of behaviour are as follows:

- ✓ No children or minors (under 18 years of age) are to be involved
- ✓ No animals are to be involved
- ✓ No scat (faeces) play

OBJECTIVES OF THE PRESENTERS

- ✓ No blood is to be let
- ✓ No permanent marking or scarring
- ✓ No knife play

However, it is up to the individual reader whether they adopt these standards of behaviour as listed above, or if they wish to create their own. The accepted conduct of all participants within any BDSM role-play session need to be agreed by all parties prior to the session. The reader must take full responsibility for any outcomes resulting from actions they take from reading this manual. The presenters cannot be held liable for the actions and the consequential outcomes of any reader following the use of this manual. (Refer back to the Disclaimer at the start of the manual).

3

Where do you stand?

This manual is directed towards novice players who are curious and want to know more and are keen on entering the BDSM fantasy world. It is also for more experienced players who are looking for new ideas or want to refine their techniques and abilities.

If this is you and you have read this far, welcome, you have come to the right place. You have identified BDSM as something you would like to experience or learn more about together with a partner.

Typically for the novice, BDSM may have strong connotations of violence and brutality based on pictures or the perception that its frequented by undesirable people practising unusual and unorthodox sexual behaviour.

Perhaps you are not yet 'sold' on the BDSM concept and will reserve judgement until you know more or have tried it at least once. And for those who have already experienced BDSM, you realise there are considerable costs involved. You may use this manual for ideas or to consider options before making significant purchases.

WHERE DO YOU STAND?

There is always the option of visiting an established parlour for a personalised session.

Given all the above, many potential players may be discouraged from making that first step and are lost to the BDSM world. This manual will benefit those who are trying to take that first step to enter the BDSM fantasy world, as well as those who have already played some scenes but feel that they need further tuition to help make their experiences safer and more enjoyable.

4

Entering the World of BDSM

There are several reasons why people become involved in the world of BDSM. Perhaps the most common is that one or both partners have had limited exposure to BDSM, and their curiosity leads them to further involvement. This initial exposure may be in the form of magazines, online, at a friend's house, or equipment and clothing in an adult shop. In these situations, the novices will often see and read extreme scenarios. These images and merchandise are most likely directed at an audience who are already experienced in BDSM activities and therefore can tolerate these scenarios.

Alternatively, the audience may want nothing more than visual entertainment. This latter category is quite content to merely read the magazines and watch the DVD's, without any thought of seriously experimenting with the content they are reading or watching. This is ok too.

When novices are unexpectedly confronted with extreme BDSM scenarios, they may react with disgust or horror at the material. This reaction is perfectly understandable.

One major obstacle for beginners is the common perception

ENTERING THE WORLD OF BDSM

that BDSM is violent and unsafe, and all the players in the scene are 'weirdos'. Because of this, many people are repelled before they even evaluate what the benefits of BDSM could be for themselves.

This manual promotes **safe, sane, and consensual** role-play. A successful BDSM relationship can be long-term and is limited only by the participants' likes and dislikes.

BBDSM role-play will bring variety into the lives of couples, particularly for those who have been together for some time. It is widely accepted that variety in sexual activities for a couple will help to keep them together for longer periods, and BDSM is an excellent method of achieving this.

Of course, BDSM is not for everyone. Like everything else, it must be tested out before being accepted as part of a couple's lives. If both partners are not in agreement that they become involved with BDSM, then they should not proceed. A common mistake is made when one partner wants to proceed, and the second partner agrees, only being motivated by wanting to keep the first partner happy. This will become an unhappy BDSM relationship, and it may have a detrimental effect on their overall relationship.

Another major obstacle for beginners is that BDSM role-play cannot be enjoyed without at least one other person involved. Invariably, this leads to individual females wondering how to get safely involved in the scene, while individual males begin frequenting BDSM parlours to satisfy their desire to become involved in serious role-play. The parlours offer good opportunities for the novice to learn using a large variety of equipment and furniture, and with a variety of experienced Dommes. In our experience, most novices prefer to conduct BDSM sessions with a consenting partner in the privacy of their own home(s) at the beginning.

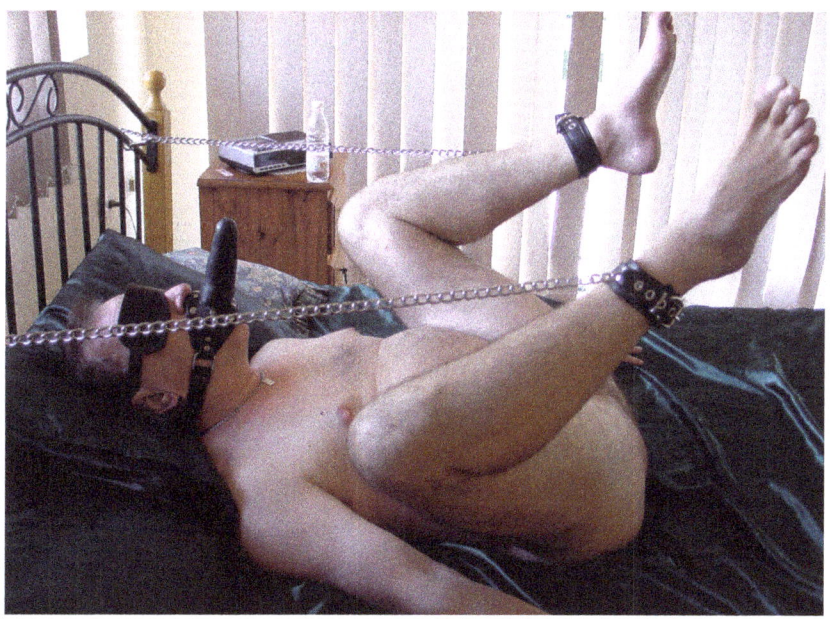

ENTERING THE WORLD OF BDSM

Let's meet our couple Mary and Fred, here is a typical scenario:

Fred is happily married to Mary. Fred has heard about bondage activities from his friends at work and is curious to find out more. He visits a sex shop close to his office and begins browsing through the endless display of magazines and DVD's dealing with different styles of BDSM. He buys one or two magazines to take back to work.

When everyone else has left the office at the end of the day, Fred takes out the magazines and reads. The magazines predominantly are filled with large glossy pictures, and text is kept to minimum (who needs a storyline with pictures like these?). The pictures are populated almost entirely by females (with all the attributes of 'Miss Universe' contestants), Fred prefers women and is not interested in men in a sexual way.

Over the following weeks and months, Fred browses through his magazines more and more. He begins adding magazines to his collection in the bottom drawer of his desk. He discovers that the pictures are causing sexual arousal, and as the weeks pass, this arousal is heightening. His solution is to rush home to Mary and make passionate love to her. This is great for Mary, and she wonders just what has caused this flurry of sexual activity in Fred lately.

In the meantime, Mary has decided that, because of Fred's recent displays of passion, she wants to spice things up a bit.

She visits a sex shop near her local shopping centre. She buys some provocative lingerie, and a vibrating dildo with all the attachments, for those long days while her man is away at the office.

While in the shop, she can't help but notice the large array of magazines with pictures of BDSM scenes. She stares, but not too intently. She dares not pick one up; just in case someone is watching, and they get the wrong idea about her. She has heard about this stuff. It's all pain and torture. All the people are weird and must be avoided at all cost. But still, her curiosity has clicked into gear.

Her problem now is that if she wanted to find out more and experiment with this stuff, just how will she go about it? She could ask the man who works in the sex shop, but she doesn't trust him. She is not very computer savvy. She could ask Fred, but what if his reaction was negative? Then she would jeopardise all the passion that has come into their lives recently. As the weeks pass, her interest diminishes, but the curiosity remains unsatisfied.

So, how do Mary and Fred resolve their individual interests in becoming involved in the BDSM scene? This type of situation is more common than most people realise. Even more common is the case where one partner has their curiosity aroused but is confronted with a partner who is oblivious to the whole scene.

Both Fred and Mary are aware and curious about the scene. Both are unaware of the other partner's feelings towards BDSM and consequently are unsure about their reactions. Obviously, to proceed, one of them must broach the subject of BDSM with the other.

For partners who have been together for some time, they should have a feeling as to how the other partner will react to the raising of the subject of BDSM. The key issue here is the partners' **trust** in each other.

In our case study, if Fred raised the idea of BDSM with Mary, it will work out fine because she is already aware of the scene and is curious to discover more.

But what if Mary knew nothing about BDSM? Fred's attitude must be that Mary trusts him, but he must not abuse that trust. He will explain everything to her and lead her gently into role-play, always giving her the option to stop at any time. Mary's attitude needs to be that she trusts Fred and knows that he will not harm her. She should be willing to at least listen to his proposal before making any final decision. If he presents a good and positive case for trying BDSM, then she may be prepared to go to the next step. After all, she should know that she can put a stop to this at any time. Once both partners have given their consent to participate, they are ready to proceed to the next step.

5

How to Start

Now that the partners have agreed they are willing to advance to the next step and begin experimenting with BDSM, quite often they will be at a loss about how to get started. If the couples are complete novices, then this manual is a perfect start for them. After reading it carefully and having a discussion about it, their next step must be to fill out the checklist found towards the end of this manual. However, if one of the partners has been oblivious to the scene until now, then the conventions need to be introduced to that partner. This will include detailing what is going to happen in the experimental role-play scenario, what equipment is going to be used, and what needs to be done when one of the partners wants to stop the experiment. The session should be short; no more than one hour. At this stage, it is a good idea for the partners to reverse their roles during the experiment so each of them can experience the sensations of performing different roles.

At the completion of the role-play, it is strongly recommended that the partners give each other feedback about how they felt, the aspects each liked or disliked, and whether it is worthwhile to continue experimenting with future sessions. If one of the partners

HOW TO START

indicates that further participation is undesirable, then this constitutes withdrawal of consent. It may be they need time to process their feelings. Communication is the key here. It could be they were triggered by a past event in which case they can go back to revise their checklist. This is the reason the checklists are crucial before a session. A sub being tied up and punished for example are at their most vulnerable, ultimately their emotional and physical health including personal safety must be respected by the Domme/Dom at all times.

The BDSM scene has its own terminology that is used on a worldwide basis. This manual uses BDSM terminology where appropriate. A Glossary of Terms has been included at the end. Some of the terms used here are self-explanatory (for example, 'role-play', 'scenes', 'scenarios', 'session' etc.).

However, it is worthwhile to briefly explain BDSM roles. The partner who is doing the actual binding and disciplining and otherwise controlling the session is referred to as the 'Dominant': 'Domme' if female, or 'Dom' if male. They can also be referred to as 'Mistress' if female, or 'Master' if male, or as 'Top' for both. The partner who is being tied up and disciplined in the session is referred to as the 'submissive', or 'sub', or 'subbie', or 'slave', or 'bottom'. Should the partners reverse their roles, this is known as 'switching', and then they have 'switch' roles. The role-play relationship between two players often is referred to as 'D/s'. This means that it is a Dominant/submissive relationship. Note that BDSM etiquette dictates that whenever a Domme/Dom is referenced, that reference must always begin with a capital letter. Consequently, whenever a sub is referenced, then that reference must always begin with a small letter. Another thing to note is there are no rules on who should take what roles, the gender of the person is not important. Although from experience, many males have a fantasy of being dominated by a female.

Participants in BDSM receive different kinds of thrills from role-play.

For the Domme/Dom, the play may be an ego trip or experimentation with
- new-found powers
- their total control over the sub
- the opportunity to use new/different equipment
- the excitement of playing out new scenarios with the sub
- sexual experimentation

For the sub, the excitement may come from:
- transferring all control to the Domme/Dom
- having bondage and discipline inflicted on them
- mind games and humiliation
- erotic sexual play

BDSM is often referred to as 'B and D'. Generally, this stands for Bondage and Discipline/ Dominance. 'S and M' implies Submission or Sadism and Masochism. Sadism is someone who inflicts pain, humiliation and suffering to another and Masochism is someone who loves to receive it.

It is this terminology that contributes to some of the misinformation about BDSM. This implies that BDSM is limited to the subs being bound and punished by the Dominant players. Sure, this happens in some part of most scenarios. However, scenarios can be made to be extremely erotic. Some erotic scenarios will be discussed involving our case study players, Mary and Fred later in this manual. An adept Dominant will be quite capable of keeping a sub at peek sexual arousal for as long as desired.

Another important aspect of BDSM is the control of the sub's senses. Once the sub is immobilised, the senses can be removed from the sub's control by using:

- ✓ A gag (to remove speech)
- ✓ A blindfold (to remove sight)

HOW TO START

- ✓ Earplugs (to remove hearing)
- ✓ Rope to bind hands (to remove touch)
- ✓ A mask or peg (to remove smell)

In this scenario, it is remarkable how a sub will react merely to the unexpected touch of a feather or an ice cube. Other interesting reactions will arise when the sub's genital area is rubbed with lubricant, or when the nipples are squeezed. In such situations, the sub cannot escape the attentions of the Dominant, and has no idea what is about to happen next (if anything). The sub has no control.

There are a multitude of experiences awaiting new players in the BDSM scene. The intensity of the scene can be set to the preference of the players. It is highly recommended that preferences should be determined by use of a **checklist** (a sample is included near the end of this manual). When the players become more comfortable in their roles, then it is most likely that their **limits** (or boundaries) will change to encompass new equipment and furniture or new ideas for role-play.

In most publications, BDSM scenes take place in well-equipped dungeons. For new players in the scene, chances are their house does not feature a dungeon with an endless array of equipment. Consequently, initial sessions most commonly take place in the main bedroom. This is quite acceptable as the initial sessions really are for experimentation without getting too serious. Atmospheric and visual effects can be introduced later, once the players commit to an ongoing involvement in the BDSM scene.

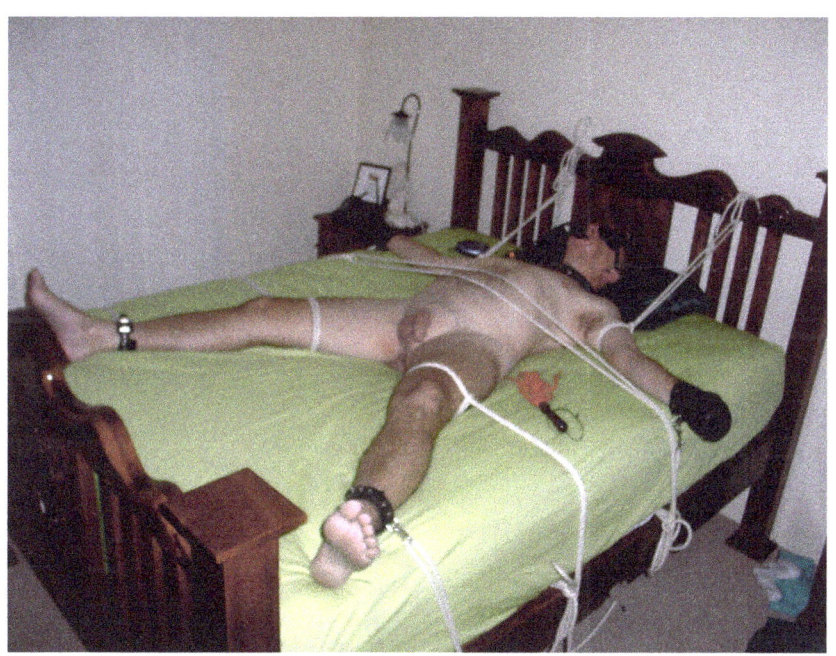

6

Use of Common Household Items

There are many common household items that can be used as 'toys' in the beginning without going on a massive equipment-buying spree.

Our case study couple Mary and Fred have decided that they are willing to experiment with a short BDSM scene where they will change roles during the session. They each fill out a checklist. They also have agreed to sit down and analyse their experiences at the end of the session, and then decide if they want to follow up with additional sessions in the future.

Ideally, they should think their session through, after discussing their individual checklists and plan the steps from start to finish. This planning is also applicable to more experienced players. It is not advisable to begin a session, then have to pause, mid-session, not knowing what to do next. The Dominant is in control and should have their objectives set and the various stages of the scenario planned. The more experienced players are able to 'ad lib' through a session, relying on their experiences. For a novice, this can be both daunting and confusing. It is common for planned sessions to not run strictly according to expectations, and often it's the little things that make a session go astray (oops, I've run out of rope!). As the players gain more experience, they will learn to adapt to these little annoyances and continue the session with a slightly modified plan. On other occasions, the Domme/Dom will think of new ways of conducting a scene in mid-session and will make adjustments accordingly based on their sub's checklist.

For beginners, aside from the checklist, a multitude of questions need to be considered and a plan put in place before beginning the first session. The questions that may arise are as follows:

- ✓ Is the sub being bound too tightly, or too loosely?
- ✓ Is the sub breathing OK?
- ✓ Is that position too uncomfortable?
- ✓ Will this table be able to take the weight of the sub?
- ✓ What do I do if I have used up all the rope?
- ✓ How hard should the sub be spanked, and for how long?
- ✓ Can the neighbours hear us?
- ✓ What if we have visitors?
- ✓ How long can the sub be left in this bound position?
- ✓ Is it OK to leave marks on the sub?

USE OF COMMON HOUSEHOLD ITEMS

All of the above may be resolved either by planning or through experience. During the first few sessions for two new role-players it is important to get the basics in place and for both to be comfortable that they are progressing in a direction that will give them enjoyment.

The next consideration for novice role-players is to determine the equipment to be used in the session. It is not recommended that novices purchase specialised bondage equipment for use in their first session. Quality equipment requires a significant investment, and it may be that after only one session, either one or both participants may not wish to proceed any further. This may be because the experience of the session was not to the players' liking, or their expectations were not met. If equipment had been purchased for this exercise, then it would be a poor investment for little or no positive return.

Are there alternatives?

There are many common household items that may be used to get new players started. With some creativity and slight modifications, makeshift items may be used in a session. Some examples are described below.

For restraints, rope is preferred. Ideally, the rope should be soft, not be too thin and should have no elasticity. If a soft rope is used, then there will be minimal damage caused to the skin of the sub. Other restraint items that could be used include men's neckties, scarves, old stockings/pantihose, and even electrical cords.

An effective gag can simply be made from placing gaffer tape, or other types of packing tape, over the mouth. Remember to check if the sub can breathe unhindered through the nose before taping over the mouth (this is not advisable if the sub has a head cold).

For a blindfold, use a sleep mask or scarf around the eyes. If the scarf is not sufficiently effective in restricting the sub's vision, then place a folded handkerchief over the eyes before tying the scarf around the head.

If a leg spreader is required, use an old broom handle modified with eye bolts at each end. (see Glossary of Terms at the end of manual for full description).

Most first-time scenarios will take place on the bed, though there are other options. A few hooks strategically placed in the frame of a doorway can lead to an interesting scenario. Also, chairs and lounges are good for forcing the sub into a position for a spanking, as is a sturdy coffee table, or even an ironing board, making sure the board is stable enough first. For spanking, the alternatives for using hands include wooden spoons and the backs of hairbrushes.

To play with the senses, use a feather or some light fabric to tickle the subject, and use ice cubes to achieve a surprising reaction. For an even more stunning reaction, use clothes pegs as nipple clamps.

There are innumerable items that may be used in a role-play scenario, and many different positions that may be augmented using household furniture. This is enough for first-timers to experience some of the sensations of BDSM. After a couple of experiments with this improvised equipment, participants should be able to decide whether to proceed further into BDSM. Then they might purchase some of the basic equipment, and maybe some suitable clothing.

Let's check on our case study couple, Fred and Mary:

> Based on each other's checklists, Fred and Mary had worked out their little scenarios individually, without telling each other their plans. They had thought about the household items, the positions to use, and the activities they would undertake during their respective half-hour as Domme/Dom. They had decided that Fred would be the Dom first, because if he went a bit too far for Mary's liking, she then had the chance to get even.
>
> Fred began by instructing Mary to get completely undressed. He blindfolded her by placing a handkerchief over her eyes and tying an old stocking around her head to keep the

blindfold in place. Next, he bound her wrists in front of her, using one of his neckties. At this point, he looped another tie around her neck and led her out into the dining room. There, he moved two dining chairs, so they stood side-by-side, leaving a small gap between them. He forced her to kneel and lean across the two seats of the chairs, with her breasts being forced into the gap between the two chairs. To achieve this, she had to shuffle forward so that her knees were no longer touching the floor and her weight was on her stomach. Using ropes from the boot of his car, he tied her thighs to the nearest legs of the first chair and tied her arms to the furthest legs of the second chair. This completed, he proceeded to give her a spanking by hand until her butt cheeks glowed a fiery red.

At the changeover of roles, they had a ten-minute break. Mary used this time to put on her new lingerie and high heels. A light touch to her makeup, and she was ready.

Mary began by ordering Fred to completely undress, and as he did so, she began a tirade of verbal abuse. Nothing he did seemed to please her. She told him to crawl across the floor and kiss her feet. She blindfolded him, using the same handkerchief and stocking that had been used on her. She tied his hands behind him, using another stocking. She positioned him at the foot of the bed, with his back to the bed, and tied each of his ankles to a leg of the bed, using two of his neckties.

He was facing the doorway towards the bathroom, Above the doorway, Mary had earlier installed a hook, which Fred had failed to notice. Using one of the ropes, she tied one end around the stocking binding his wrists behind him. She passed the rope up over his head, through the hook above the doorway, with the end of the rope to be tied to the doorknob. To her delight, she discovered that as the rope was drawn towards the hook, Fred's bound wrists were raised, and he was forced to bend forward. She pulled on the rope until she had the desired position. She returned the compliment of being spanked. It wasn't long before she found her hand hurting. This was quickly solved by taking the wide belt from Fred's jeans on the floor and using the belt as a strap. His buttocks were soon glowing. Mary was laughing!

After showering, Mary and Fred discussed their experiences. Mary claimed that she enjoyed disciplining Fred, and that her plan with the hook worked better than she had expected. Fred said he enjoyed the feeling of helplessness and humiliation immensely. Both agreed that further experiments were in order.

In this case study, the scenarios enacted were simplistic and items found in the home were used. Experiments like this will be enough for beginners to be able to determine if they want to continue experimenting with future sessions. Also, as Fred and Mary discussed the session, their preferred roles began to evolve.

7

Defining Your Relationship

When a new Dom/sub relationship is formed, it is recommended that the relationship should be clearly defined with a checklist of preferences and dislikes. For the longer-term, serious relationships, a detailed **agreement** should be drawn up and signed. An example agreement may be found at the end of this manual.

For this D/s relationship to work, it must be decided if this is to be a:

- ✓ **24/7 (full-time)** lifestyle for both Dom and sub
- ✓ **24/7 (on-call)** lifestyle with total control transferrable, as required
- ✓ **Casual Dom/sub** relationship (whenever it is mutually agreed upon)

For the **24/7 full-time** arrangement, there are numerous considerations, particularly for the dominant partner, to consider. Some of these considerations include, but are not limited to:

- ✓ Out-of-role time for the sub

- ✓ Sleeping arrangements
- ✓ Eating arrangements
- ✓ Clothing
- ✓ Interactions with associates of the Domme/Dom (e.g. family, business associates)
- ✓ Activities outside the home (e.g. holidays)

Out-of-role time must be provided for 24/7 full-time subs. It is not reasonable to expect the sub to remain totally without some personal time. Each day, personal time should be allowed to the sub so that normal daily activities (e.g. using the bathroom) may be conducted. Enough time must be allowed for these activities to prevent the sub from 'burning out'. This applies to subs who are in role for more than two days (although this period is arbitrary, depending on the participants). If subs are not granted enough personal time, they will become increasingly disenchanted with the role-play, and they will be looking for an early conclusion rather than enjoying their current role. It is unlikely that such subs would enter further scenarios with that particular Domme/Dom.

DEFINING YOUR RELATIONSHIP

Sleeping arrangements for the sub can vary at the discretion of the Domme/Dom. The sub may be allocated their own bed and bedroom, or they may be provided with a blanket on the floor at the foot of the Domme/Dom's bed, or they may be ordered to sleep in a cage. These arrangements depend on the other activities that the Domme/Dom has planned for the sub. For example, if the Domme/Dom expects the sub to perform sexual favours during the night, or expects the sub to rise very early to begin heating the house and preparing breakfast, then it is not practical to have the sub locked in a cage for the night (unless the Domme/Dom is prepared to get out of bed to let the sub out of the cage to perform the required tasks).

Eating arrangements for the sub can vary at the whim of the Domme/Dom. Perhaps the sub may be required to live on a restricted diet, as defined by the Domme/Dom. Or maybe the sub must eat their meals out in the kitchen, after the Domme/Dom (and guests?) have finished eating in the dining room. Perhaps the sub must eat their meals on the floor under the dining table, possibly with their hands bound behind the back, while eating from a dog bowl. Or maybe the sub will be allowed to eat at the same table as the Domme/Dom without utensils. Maybe there will be a mixture of all these situations, depending on the level of the intensity of the relationship in force at that particular time. (See specific activities and example scenarios near the end of the manual)

Clothing for a sub will vary depending on the situation. Standard household attire for a sub is a latex G-string for a female or latex jock strap for a male. This is totally inappropriate dress if the Domme/Dom wishes to take the sub to the local supermarket. If the sub is female, it might be interesting to dress her in slutty

DEFINING YOUR RELATIONSHIP

clothing and take her to a classy restaurant at night, or to walk her around a 'red light' district in town. If the sub is male, an interesting scenario might be to fully cross dress him as a maid and have him wait on the table of the Domme/Dom and guests. In all these scenarios, the subs could also be wearing a chastity belt with plugs attached. (see Glossary of Terms at the end of this manual)

The Domme/Dom must remember that the sub has no right to decide the attire at any time, therefore, clothing for the sub's given situation must be a consideration for the Domme/Dom.

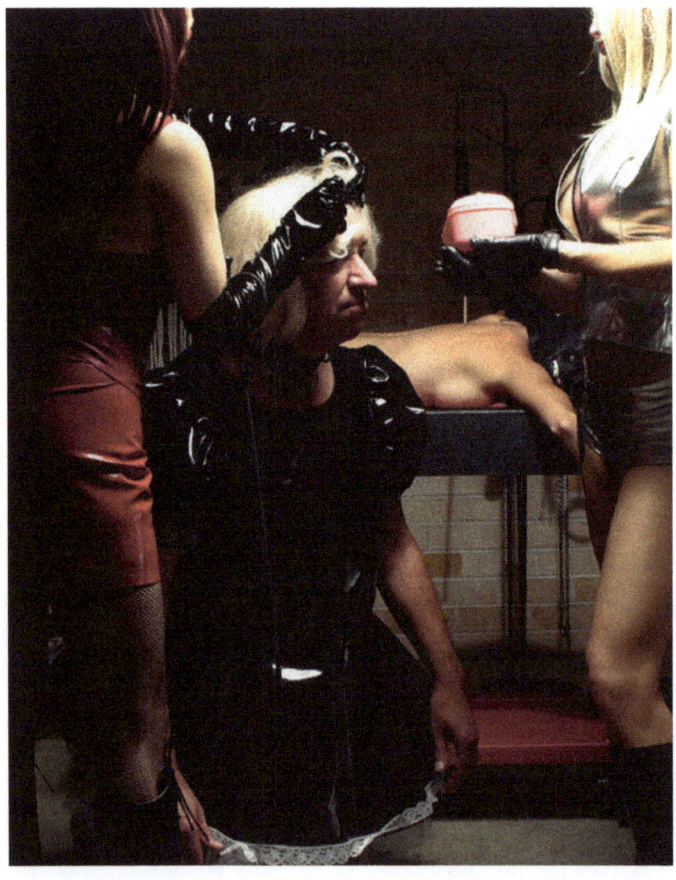

Interactions with associates of the Domme/Dom will be dictated depending on nature of the associates, and if they are aware of the D/s relationship, and/or the BDSM activities of the Domme/Dom. The interactions will also depend on the current level of intensity of the role-play.

Activities outside the home are similar to interactions with associates. The nature of these activities will be dependant on the role-play being undertaken.

There are many situations that a Domme/Dom and sub will have to navigate while they are in role-play together on a 24/7 basis. Much of this involves being confronted by people who may or may not know anything of the roles being enacted before their eyes. It may be that the Domme/Dom wants these people to know of the relationship, or maybe the other people are to be kept oblivious to the roles and situations. The best way of controlling this is to use defined levels of intensity for the entire period of the role-play. The levels must be given to and learnt by the sub on day one of the role-play.

Some examples of **levels of intensity** are as follows:

- ✓ **Level One:**
  This includes personal time allocated to the sub at the discretion of the Domme/Dom. The D/s relationship still is very much in existence, this level allows the sub to tend to personal activities without the Domme/Dom standing behind and watching, with their whip in hand.

- ✓ **Level Two:**
  To all onlookers, there appears to be nothing out of the ordinary when players are using this level. The

sub is dressed in their everyday wear (although there could be some interesting toys being utilised under the clothing), and the sub acts normally and joins in conversations as expected. The Domme/Dom could keep track of the sub's performance in these situations, with 'indiscretions' and 'mistakes' being punished when they return to the 'normal' D/s environment. In these level two situations, the Domme/Dom wishes to keep the details of the role-play absolutely hidden from the onlookers, visitors, etc. Any slip-up by the sub will most likely cause considerable embarrassment for the Domme/Dom and sub will have to be punished accordingly. Typical onlookers in this category would be the Domme/Dom's parents or other family members, or perhaps the staff at the local bank where the Domme/Dom is well-known and respected.

✓ **Level Three:**
This is similar to level two except the Domme/Dom may wish to disclose the D/s relationship to others. Again, this is at the total discretion of the Domme/Dom. And when that decision is made, quite often it will be an exercise in humiliation for the sub.

For example, the Domme/Dom and sub are walking down the street. Level two intensity could have been in force. But the Domme/Dom is not sure if they may meet some acquaintances, so level three is imposed on the sub. Sure enough, in the main shopping centre, they happen to meet some of the Domme/Dom's friends, and immediately the sub is instructed to greet them by kissing their feet. No doubt this activity will cause interested stares from passers-by, and will cause deserved humility and embarrassment for the sub. If the sub does not perform to the satisfaction of the Domme/Dom, the sub will be punished upon returning to the 'dungeon'.

✓ **Level Four:**
This level is for use when the sub is to be in full submissive role, dressed (or undressed) appropriately. The sub may be wearing restrictive items such as a gag, hand cuffs, leg cuffs, dildo, butt plug, nipple clamps, and/or chastity belt. This is also the level for light-to-medium discipline and humiliation. Typically, this is the level to use when the sub is expected to perform standard household chores, prepare meals, and/or provide drinks and snacks for the Domme/Dom.

✓ **Level Five:**
One step up from a level four situation, level five is reserved for heavier disciplining sessions, such as a caning or a whipping while the sub is securely bound. This may be a ritual daily event, or it may be in response to some less than satisfactory performances by the sub. Alternatively, it may be that the Domme/Dom merely wishes to improve Her/His techniques, or to try out some new equipment. It is always more interesting when there are spectators to these sessions.

✓ **Level Six:**
This level is reserved only for severe or extreme bondage and discipline. This may be the result of the Domme/Dom's extreme displeasure at something the sub has done, or not done. Alternatively, the Domme/Dom may simply want to test the limits of the sub, and to push the sub's boundaries a little further.

DEFINING YOUR RELATIONSHIP

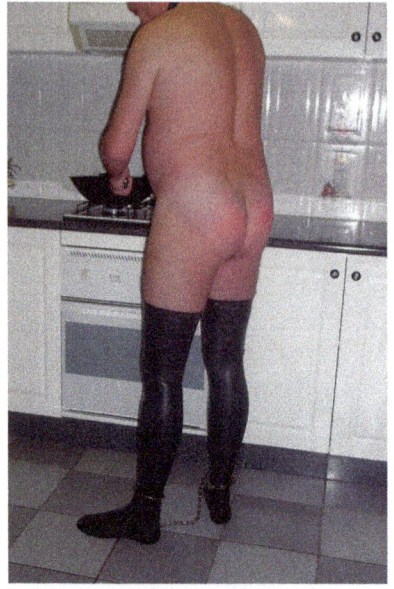

For **24/7 full-time** relationships, the Domme/Dom has ample time to develop protocols and procedures for the sub, thus moving in a defined direction for the training of the sub according to the requirements of the Domme/Dom, and possibly the sub. Targets should be defined, with the sub receiving appropriate rewards for progressing towards those targets, or appropriate punishment for non-achievement. One target for any Domme/Dom/sub relationship must be an **immediate and unquestioning response** to any command given by the Domme/Dom. While this may appear to be obvious and simple, it is something that novice subs will have to work towards. This is not always an easy task.

A 24/7 on-call relationship is self-explanatory, the amount of notice must be defined. Perhaps this kind of relationship can be undertaken at pre-arranged times (e.g. every second weekend). The situation of a 24/7 on-call relationship is like that of the full-time arrangement. The obvious difference is in the length of the relationship; however, all of the rules and activities still apply to this shorter relationship.

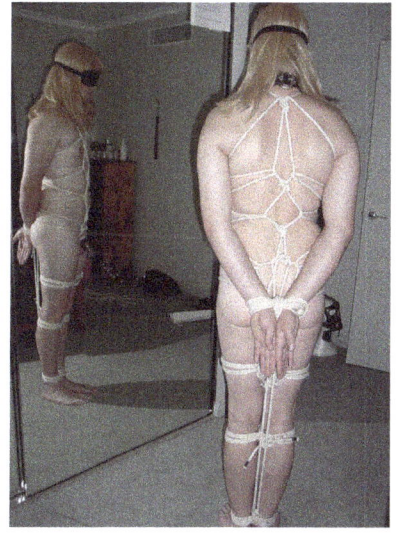

Casual submissives are usually activated on an 'as required' basis. Quite often sessions with them will be set up to experiment with a piece of equipment, or within a scenario. These are usually session visits of one to four hours in duration. It is highly recommended that prior to this type of session, the participants clearly define what is required and expected of each other based also on the checklist activities. This negotiating must be done outside of the role-play.

Professional Mistress is the supplier, paid for the service, to satisfy the requirements of the sub over the period of the session.

8

Safe Words and General Safety

Any successful D/s (Dominant/submissive) relationship will generate a bond (no pun intended) of trust between the participants.

It is the responsibility of the Domme/Dom to develop this trust to a point where the sub will accept any instructions or activities from the Domme/Dom without question and without hesitation. These instructions include specifications relating to behaviour in the home and in public, mode of dress, diet, general subservience, and acceptance of any punishments.

Once this level of trust has been reached, this becomes an extremely valuable and satisfying relationship for both parties. This situation is the ultimate aim of any D/s relationship.

No matter the level of trust that exists, or the status of the relationship, it is essential that a method of signals be established so that the sub can indicate problems to the Domme/Dom. The sub can experience sudden and unexpected problems such as cramping or breathing difficulties (e.g. coughing or sneezing while gagged).

BOUND FOR PLAY - BDSM TRAINING MANUAL

SAFE WORDS AND GENERAL SAFETY

A **safe word** must be established between the Domme/Dom and sub, before any role-play begins. If a gag is being used, then some other easily noticeable signal (such as violent shaking of the head or jumping up and down). If the Domme/Dom is about to restrict the sub with gag and bind them in such a way to prevent movement of the head or jumping, then the Domme/Dom is responsible for confirming the safe word or signal before bounding the sub in a restrictive position. It is important that the sub understands this before proceeding with the bondage position. The use of the **safe word** or signal must bring all activities to an immediate stop so that the sub can convey the problem to the Domme/Dom. Activities may be resumed once the problem is corrected.

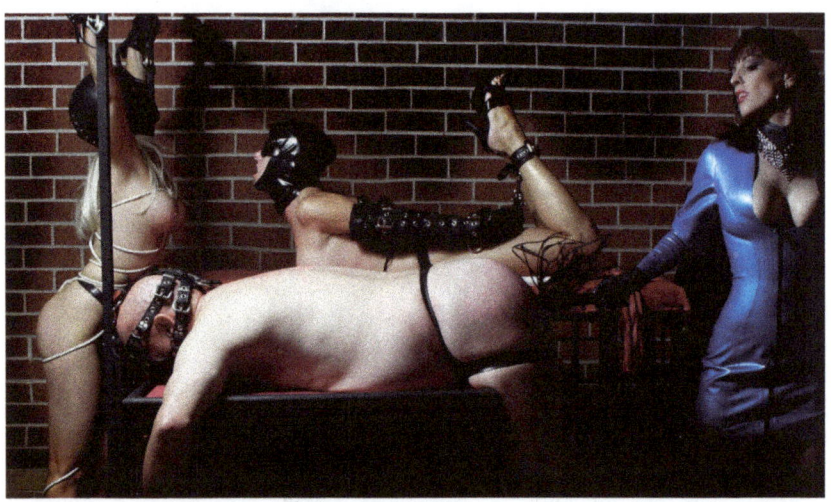

It is not advisable to use words such as 'no', 'no more', 'help' as the **safe words** as these can often be used in part of the role-play scenario (e.g. in a fantasy scene).

An alternative to the **safe word** is the traffic light system using the colours red and orange. In this situation, red means: 'Stop! The sub has a serious problem!', orange means sub wants to stay in role but change the intensity or scenario. This is not to say sub is in control during roleplay because Domme/Dom may only lighten the intensity of the bondage/punishment if orange is the signal, this is at the discretion of the Domme/Dom. The Domme/Dom sets up the roleplay based on the subs checklist of preferences they completed at the start of the session. However, in reality the sub IS in control of the session in terms of stopping the session or shifting it to another scene if they feel uncomfortable.

As a reminder, IT IS ESSENTIAL THAT DRUGS AND ALCOHOL BE BANNED FROM USE BEFORE AND DURING SESSIONS. Dommes/Doms under the influence of drugs and/or alcohol pose a very serious threat to their subs when their judgement is impaired, while the subs under the influence may be unable to assess the seriousness of problems as they occur.

9

Hygiene

As with safety, hygiene is an aspect of paramount importance. When a new long-term relationship is formed, it is advisable for participants to undergo sexual health tests before beginning any intimate role-play scenarios. The most critical of these are tests for HIV and Hepatitis-C. Before commencing a session, it is also strongly advised that all participants be given the opportunity to examine each other for other health issues such as genital herpes.
subs must also make known to the Domme/Dom any general health problems they may have. This will include things such as asthma, head colds, heart related issues, muscular and arthritic problems.

It is pertinent to advise that for any equipment that is inserted into the body or equipment that may be shared by others (such as gags, dildos and butt plugs), adequate protection must be provided using condoms, (so what if a sub gets a condom in the mouth and not the taste of leather or rubber?). Disinfecting these items after session is an absolute must including a clean and wipe down of all equipment as well. Hygiene of individual pieces of equipment will be explained in chapter twenty-three.

In addition, whenever any form of anal play is part of the scenario, the Domme/Dom is advised to wear surgical latex gloves. Any dildos, plugs and gags inserted must have condoms on them. Prior to anal play taking place, at least one enema should be administered to the sub for cleansing purposes.

10

Consent

The object of any role-play relationship is to provide maximum enjoyment to all participants. The other important aspect is the consent of the participating parties, particularly the consent of any submissives involved in the role-play.

Without the appropriate consent of the subs, the whole scenario will fail. The role-play will degenerate into an atmosphere where the sub is forced to perform against his/her wishes. This is a dangerous situation, and it can never work. It is advisable to terminate the relationship where there is an absence of full consent.

Consent should be determined at the very initiation of the session. For longer term 24/7 sessions, it should be covered in an agreement between the parties (example of an agreement can be found at the end of this manual). For short-term or casual scenarios, consent must be clearly defined, including the checklist for all activities within the planned scenario.

Usually, consent is in direct proportion to the amount of **trust** that the sub has in the Domme/Dom. If it is a new relationship, then the sub may be reluctant to grant consent to the more extreme activities. However, if it is an established relationship, the sub may be expected to give consent to the Domme/Dom to conduct the scenario with whatever activities are planned providing that the sub's pre-defined **limits** are respected.

The sub may advise the Domme/Dom that permission is given to perform certain activities, but not others. This will be noted in the checklist before the session. If the Domme/Dom proceeds with the scenario, but then disregards the requests of the sub, then there will be a breakdown in the level of **trust.** This is a serious breach in the relationship and may lead to total failure of an ongoing relationship.

It is the responsibility of the Domme/Dom to ensure that the sub consents to activities before they are introduced to a session. And, if the sub has objections or requests as per the checklist, then the Domme/Dom is obliged to honour these once the session has commenced.

11

Limits

Irrespective of the level of experience of the submissive, usually there are some activities in which the sub does not want to participate. These must be clearly identified at the beginning of the relationship, either verbally or in a written agreement. Once these have been accepted and agreed to by the Domme/Dom, then the limits of the sub must always be respected.

The sub must reserve the right to alter her/his limits at any time outside of the role-play session.

Alternatively, the Domme/Dom may indicate to the sub that although She/He acknowledges the sub's limits, She/He wants to push those limits to new boundaries. This activity should only be introduced with the consent of the sub. It is likely after this event that the sub will change the existing limits depending on sub's enjoyment or not. Quite often, this is a challenge for both participants. This is also where the safe word is most commonly used.

In other situations, a sub may state that there are no limits at all. This is not a licence for the Domme/Dom to run amok. Indeed, this situation requires the Domme/Dom to be more astute in assessing how far the sub may be involved in the various activities

in the session planned by the Domme/Dom. In this case, the role-players will need to rely on the established safe word.

Also, it is acceptable for the Domme/Dom to impose their own limits on session activities. Even though the sub may want a certain activity, the Domme/Dom reserves the right not to perform this. After all, it is the Domme/Dom who is in control here!

For short-term or casual relationships, it is advisable to review planned activities with the sub, thus determining their limits for the planned session. For longer-term relationships such as a 24/7, it is advisable to take the sub through a checklist of activities to determine the sub's limits and interests.

12

Checklist

An ideal method for the Domme/Dom to determine the experiences and expectations of the sub is to use a checklist. Several forms of activity checklists are available on various sites on the internet or there is an example of one at the end of this manual. Whichever one is ultimately used, there are some requirements that should be included on any checklist. A general section should include the sub's name and the date that the checklist was completed. It should also include some guidance to filling out the bulk of the checklist.

The main body of the checklist must list all possible activities. It is worthwhile listing even those activities that are outside the limits of the Domme/Dom. The sub is still expected to respond to these activities.

For each of the activities, the sub will need to indicate any experience with each activity, the willingness to participate in each activity, and to comment on each activity if needed. The option to answer each question simply should be a 'yes', 'no', or an 'N/A' (meaning not applicable to gender).

The options for defining an individual's willingness to perform or be subjected to an activity should be:

5   Wild turn on – as often as possible please
4   I like doing this on a regular basis
3   I usually like this on an occasional basis
2   I am willing to do this, but it has no special appeal
1   I don't like this but won't object if asked to do it
0   I don't like this and will object – I will only do this if the Domme/Dom really wants it
NO I will not do this under any circumstances
?   I don't understand what this is, Domme/Dom to explain

Comments by the sub on each of the activities should be encouraged.

13

Agreement

For longer-term 24/7 relationships, it is common to have a contract drawn up and signed by both Domme/Dom and sub. Note that this is not intended to be a legally binding agreement, its purpose is to state very clearly, for both parties, the guidelines for the proposed relationship.

Agreements should be drawn up considering each individual sub and the role that is intended for them. Aspects to be covered by the agreement include:

- ✓ slave's role
- ✓ slave's general behaviour
- ✓ slave's dress/body/appearance
- ✓ Domme/Dom's role
- ✓ Punishment
- ✓ Other people
- ✓ Alterations to agreement
- ✓ Termination of agreement
- ✓ slave's signature
- ✓ Domme/Dom's signature

A sample of a slavery agreement is appended at the end of this manual.

14

Clothing

Whether the Domme/Dom is operating in a professional capacity, or merely for private enjoyment with a sub, clothing is a most important consideration. Clothing can significantly contribute to the mood and atmosphere of a session.

For a Mistress (Domme), there is a popular conception about the way a Mistress should look, her personal appearance and clothing style. This perception has evolved from a multitude of magazines and videos, and now has become something of a default image, particularly for professional Mistresses. subs who are paying for session time with the Mistress will not participate if the Mistress does not fit into their perceived image of a professional

Mistress. It is most disconcerting when the sub knocks on the door of the Mistress, and She answers the door wearing a dressing gown with her hair in rollers!

In any roleplay scenario, the expectations dictate that the professional Mistress will be dressed in suitable clothing for the role and generally wearing heavy makeup. Clothing will be leather, PVC, or latex. While clothing should be revealing and/or tightfitting, it must also be practical and comfortable for the Mistress to work in during the session (e.g. a heavily boned corset may look great, but  novices need to bear in mind it may be a little difficult to effectively move around in the session). Footwear should be boots or shoes with high heels. If a Mistress was to appear in session wearing pastel-coloured lingerie and flat shoes, no sub would be impressed, nor will she be taken seriously in the session. The Domme/sub relationship will break down.

The clothing requirements for a private Mistress (particularly with a 24/7 sub) are not so demanding, although a session in the dungeon with the sub should be conducted with the preferred image of a confident Mistress (as described above).

For a Master (Dom), the image is less defined. However, the air of superiority and control can be assisted by the appearance of the Master. Leathers and latex are suitable and flexible wear for the Master in His dungeon. Obviously, less formal wear will be required around the house in a 24/7 relationship.

CLOTHING

For both Mistresses and Masters, it is advisable to wear clothing that is clean, undamaged, tidy, and functional, particularly for intense sessions in the dungeon. This will enhance an image of Dominance over the submissive(s). Alternatively, should the Domme/Dom wear dirty boots or smeared latex into a session, it can become the sub's task to clean these items while still being worn by the Domme/Dom.

Perhaps the Domme's/Dom's choice of attire will be dictated by a scenario being played (e.g. Doctor/patient, Teacher/student, etc.). Even in these situations, the standards mentioned above still will apply.

Clothing for a sub is optional, particularly in a dungeon session, and is purely at the discretion of the Domme/Dom. Attire for scenes outside of the dungeon will vary greatly, depending on the roles as dictated by the Domme/Dom. For example, a sub (of either gender) may be dressed as a maid for household chores, or as a slut for public exhibition, or dressed in only a loose shirt so that all parts of the sub's body are easily accessible to Domme/Dom on demand.

A sub does not have the luxury of deciding the clothing to wear at any time or in any situation. These are decisions to be made only by the Domme/Dom.

It is also the Domme/Dom's decision regarding the 24/7 sub's personal appearance. For example, the Domme/Dom may decide that the sub must alter their hairstyle and/or colour, or maybe the hair must be shaved off altogether.

15

Appearance

Although it may seem to be an insignificant point, the appearance of the Domme/Dom does have considerable impact on a session, or on a longer-term relationship.

The Domme/Dom must maintain an air of superiority, confidence, and control when in the presence of submissives. This will become more natural as the Domme/Dom gains experience and builds self-confidence. Once this superiority, confidence, and control are degraded, the whole relationship is jeopardised, unless this is corrected immediately. An indication of such degradation may be the submissive topping from the bottom (where the submissive influences the activities and direction during the session).

When done correctly, the Domme/Dom will develop a style, although this may vary from sub to sub. Various attitudes may be used by the Domme/Dom to best fit the scenario being played out. For example, the approach used for an interrogation and disciplinary session will be totally different to the approach used for a domestic duties' session. In both scenarios, the control of the Domme/Dom must be absolute.

When combined with dress codes (as discussed previously), the control and style of the Domme/Dom builds towards the appearance of absolute power over the submissive. This is an all-important psychological advantage for the Domme/Dom in the role-playing scenario.

The appearance of the submissives must always be at the discretion of the Domme/Dom. Particularly in a 24/7 relationship, where sub has given over full control, it is the Domme/Dom who will decide the sub's clothing, how they will maintain their physical appearance, what they eat and when, what they say and how and to whom, and when they will sleep. Combined, these two roles build a powerful relationship.

16

Body Language

The Domme/Dom will train the sub to behave to the individual requirements of the Domme/Dom, and behaviour may vary from sub to sub, often depending on the personalities, temperaments, and roles of the individual subs. It is the ultimate objective for the sub to obey the Domme/Dom without hesitation and without question. Eventually, the sub will be able to anticipate the requirements of the Domme/Dom, and will provide the appropriate services, according to the accepted routines.

However, Dommes/Doms must remain vigilant for any signs of dissent from the sub. Often the earliest signs of a problem can be detected by observing the sub's body language. Possible indications include the sub closing or clenching the fists, keeping toes flexed while in a kneeling position, keeping the mouth tightly closed, keeping legs pressed together, or not making all parts of the body freely available to the Domme/Dom. In addition, some facial expressions and bodily gestures can also be indicators of potential problems. A competent Domme/Dom will observe these signs for what they really are and will address the behaviour to avert any possible serious breakdown in the relationship.

Dommes/Doms must ensure the sub understands what is physically required from them in various situations and scenarios. Unless this understanding is established, the body language signs will be misconstrued. This may take a period of time but comes under the general heading of 'slave training'. Really, this works best with effective communication, which ultimately results in both experiencing an enjoyable role-play session.

17

BDSM vs. Abuse

The key difference between BDSM and abuse is consent. Consent implies an individual's agreement with the activities proposed or enacted by another. Abuse is injuring or damaging the other party without consent.

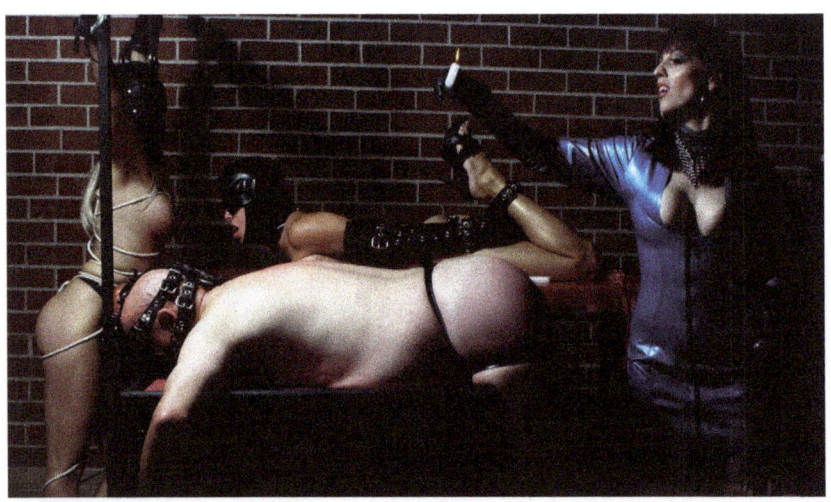

Below is a table of comparisons:

BDSM:	Abuse:
Based on safe, sane, consensual	Not negotiated
Controlled environment	Out of controlled environment
Safe words to stop the scenario	No safe words
Domme/Dom looks after well-being of sub	Does not care about sub
Can be an erotic sexual encounter	Always one-sided
Both partners are enjoying themselves	No one enjoys the results
Respects the limits of the sub	Performs non-consensual violence
Mutual respect	No respect from either party
Relationship is fulfilling	Both parties are left unfulfilled
Both feel they contribute to relationship	Domme/Dom feels they are superior
One can ask their partner to 'play'	A person does not ask for abuse
Relationship is based on trust	No trust between partners
A sub voluntarily serves the Domme/Dom	Dom does not care about consent
Is about building trust	Has no trust
Builds self esteem	Destroys self esteem
Builds the spirit of a sub	Destroys the spirit of the sub

BDSM VS. ABUSE

Dommes/Doms should be aware of the following possibilities:

- ✓ A sub may be in 'sub space' and not have the presence of mind to stop the scenario. **Watch for the sub's wellbeing.**
- ✓ Recalling, also known as flashbacks, can lead to complex situations. For example, a sub who had suffered a traumatic experience years ago, might recall this moment during a humiliation scene. **This possibility could be mentioned to sub before a session. This is the reason the checklist is important before a session. Remind them they can stop the session at any time using the safe word.**
- ✓ Always use common sense. You are playing with a human being who has given you the gift of trust. **Don't abuse that trust!**
- ✓ Reputation takes a lifetime to earn yet can be lost in a second. **For a moment of gratification, don't ruin someone's life.**

18

Roles and Names

The roles of the individuals in BDSM scenarios are easily defined, unless any of the role-players has elected to be a switch, and this has been agreed by the Domme/Dom involved.

A switch is a role-player who may take either Dommc/Dom or sub role depending on the scenario being played out at the time. A switch may do so because:

- ✓ She/He cannot decide on which role is most suitable for them
- ✓ She/He has had experience as a sub, but now wants to change roles, and does so on a programmed learning basis under the guidance of the Domme/Dom.

It is worth noting that many players will have difficulty in switching roles within a session. It is not advisable to switch midway through a session unless both parties discuss and agree to do so beforehand. This may be possible when novice players choose to conduct a one-hour session, and both agree after half hour they come out of role and switch. For both the Dominant and submissive roles, the players need

ROLES AND NAMES

to mentally prepare themselves for the roles they are playing. subs often will enter 'sub space' when they are devoted to their role. This is a condition where, mentally, they are taken into the fantasy life of the submissive character they are playing, like an actor on stage.

Obviously, it becomes quite difficult to drop that persona and adopt a Dominant character in a matter of minutes. A similar situation applies for the Dominant character, although this role demands they must always remain highly alert, looking out particularly after the wellbeing of the submissive in the role scenario. Consequently, it is easier to switch roles from session to session, and not in mid session.

It is highly recommended that novice Dommes/Doms should gain experience in a submissive role before taking on the responsibilities of being the Dominant partner. The Domme/Dom must have total control over activities, and this includes knowledge of the actions being done to the sub. Not only does the Domme/Dom need to have the knowledge of how to apply various forms of restriction and discipline, they must be aware of the effect of their actions on the sub. Ideally, the Domme/Dom must know the effects of the discipline being applied and the feeling of being put into the various bondage positions.

This can only be achieved by taking a sub role, usually early in their role-playing. This is a period of obtaining invaluable knowledge and experience, and it will prove to be of immense value to the Domme/Dom when controlling a session over a sub. It is always vital that the Domme/Dom be aware of the sub's condition during sessions.

When new equipment or furniture is purchased, the Domme/Dom should experiment with these first, so they know the feeling the sub will experience.

Accurate monitoring of the sub's condition will contribute towards a long, trusting and rewarding D/s relationship. When a sub meets a new Domme/Dom who claims they don't need this type of experience, then the sub's reaction will be one of uncertainty and mistrust.

Generally, the allocation of role names is the responsibility of the Domme/Dom, although this may be done in consultation with the sub for the sub's name. Derogatory names may be used for subs. For example, it may be necessary for the Domme/Dom to speak to the sub by name and in public. The public may not understand the reason the Domme/Dom calls the sub as 'slut' or 'cum-bucket' or 'drippy dick', while in a supermarket or in a queue at the bank. While this may be considered a form of public humiliation for the sub, the reactions of the public must be considered in these types of scenarios. It can be assumed that the unsuspecting public will view this behaviour very poorly.

ROLES AND NAMES

There are several scenarios that have become a standard in BDSM role-play, but really, the role-play is only limited by the imaginations of the players. Some of these scenarios include, but are not limited to:

- ✓ **Teacher and student:** The student is interrogated and punished for several misdemeanours such as failing exams, failing to complete homework, attempted sexual activity in the schoolyard, etc.
- ✓ **Doctor/nurse and patient:** The patient is placed on an examination table for a detailed body examination by a doctor or nurse (or both), because of the intimate nature of the examination, the patient will need to be restrained.
- ✓ **Policeman/policewoman and suspect:** The suspect is interrogated by police for several offences and is punished accordingly.
- ✓ **Army officer and enemy prisoner:** The prisoner is interrogated by an army officer regarding enemy activities and is tortured to extract information.

Clothing for all these scenarios are readily available in sex shops or online. However, role-play is not limited to these scenarios, and new scenes can be made easily by Dommes/Doms who are creative. Some examples may be:

- ✓ The sub has hands bound behind back and is blindfolded, then must move about the room/house locating various items as nominated by the Domme/Dom. Failure to do so within a prescribed time limit incurs severe punishment.
- ✓ The sub has hands bound behind back and ankles bound to thighs, and then is forced to walk on knees around a prescribed course. Failure to do so within a

prescribed time limit incurs severe punishment.
- ✓ The sub is asked a series of common knowledge questions (e.g. from Trivial Pursuit). For each incorrect answer, one item of bondage is added to the sub, and for each two correct answers, one item of bondage is removed. Once all items are on the sub, and still incorrect answers are given, then severe punishment will be inflicted.

These examples are simple but can be a lot of fun. It is even more fun if there is more than one sub involved, and they are placed into a competitive situation.

Some examples of full scenarios are covered at the end of the manual.

19

Professional vs. Private/Casual BDSM Activities

Many role-playing scenarios take place in a private environment, where the Domme/Dom controls the actions, the role play, and the activities based on their sub's checklist. Often, there will be a personal **trust** between the role-players, based on experiences from previous sessions.

However, in a professional environment, the submissive becomes a client of the Domme/Dom, and usually, it is the submissive who will dictate the scenario based on the checklist they fill out before the session begins. Here, the Domme/Dom becomes the supplier of a service to satisfy the requirements of the submissive over the period of the session. Generally, sessions are short-term only, so often a relationship does not develop, unless the submissive visits the Domme/Dom for repeated sessions.

The Domme/Dom in the professional scenario must always present a professional Dominant image, even though this image may be dictated by the requirements of the submissive client. This is evident where the client requests the Domme/Dom to play a particular role to satisfy the fantasy of the client.

Whether this is a professional or a private relationship, the

Domme/Dom still has the responsibility for the wellbeing of the submissive. The submissive is expecting the Domme/Dom to accept that responsibility and to provide activities taking into account **hygiene and safety,** while acknowledging any out-of-session instructions **(limits)** from the submissive.

Both types of environments are successful only when all parties concerned are dedicated to playing their allocated roles.

Physical vs. Mental Activities

To the uninitiated, BDSM activities seem principally to be physical activities by both the Domme/Dom and the sub. Often, BDSM is perceived as various actions revolving around restraint and punishment (commonly referred to as bondage and discipline).

However, it is worth considering the mental aspects of the typical BDSM relationship. It is the aim of the Domme/Dom to train the submissive so that the Domme/Dom maintains total control over the sub's body and mind. This is particularly relevant to a 24/7 relationship.

It is the ideal to have the sub responding to situations by 'second nature', without hesitation, and without question. Here, the Domme/Dom has established total control over the mind of the sub. The sub will accept this, and place complete **trust** in the decisions and requests of the Domme/Dom. Even without direct commands, the sub will know what is expected, and will wait in various positions and locations favoured by the Domme/Dom.

Of course, physical activities may still be an integral part of the relationship. These can take the form of restraint, punishment, or other activities such as humiliation, public exhibitionism or erotic sexual play. Always, these are at the discretion of the Domme/Dom. So, it becomes the responsibility of the Domme/Dom to plan appropriate activities for the role-players to enact.

Another significant aspect of the mental control involved is the deliberate withholding of information from the sub. This removes the sub's control over the situations and subsequent activities of the sub. It also increases the sub's dependence and **trust** on the Domme/Dom. For example, the sub may be told to dress as a maid and to serve guests at the Domme/Dom's dinner party, but the sub is not told if the guests are BDSM-aware. There are a multitude of scenarios along this theme, all of which will continue to establish in the mind of the sub just what a lowly position she/he occupies in the household of their Domme/Dom.

All role-playing scenarios can be set up by the Domme/Dom without any prior knowledge of the sub. This keeps the relationship active and interesting to both parties.

The mental control of a sub, particularly in the long-term relationships, can be more effective and more important than any of the physical aspects of the BDSM scene.

PHYSICAL VS. MENTAL ACTIVITIES

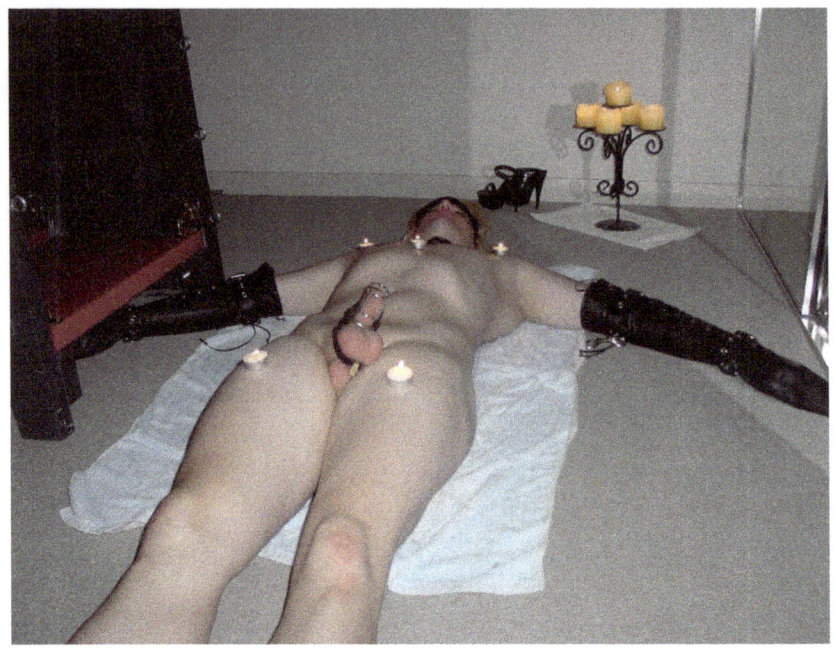

21

Full-time 24/7 Sessions

Standard short-term sessions last anywhere up to four hours. Anything beyond this may be regarded as a long-term session. A full-time 24/7 session may be overnight (e.g. from 8pm to 8am), weekend (from 8pm Friday to 8pm Sunday), or for a few days (and nights).

Such sessions bring added (and obvious) responsibilities to the Domme/Dom.

For full-time 24/7 sessions, the Domme/Dom now has to consider other factors on behalf of the submissive. These include, but are not limited to:

- ✓ Food and drink – what, when, how?
- ✓ Sleep – where, when, how long?
- ✓ Rest – break from role-playing?
- ✓ Bathroom use – how often, what use, privacy?
- ✓ Intensity of treatment/punishment

The Domme/Dom must be aware of additional strain (physically and mentally) on the sub. Extended sessions may have unexpected

FULL-TIME 24/7 SESSIONS

effects on the submissive (even unexpected to the sub), particular conditions to be wary of include, but are not limited to:

- ✓ Breathing difficulties
- ✓ Allergies
- ✓ Circulation problems
- ✓ Known health problems (heart, asthma, head cold, etc.)
- ✓ Dietary requirements
- ✓ Restrictions on sleep, food, and drink

Should any difficulties be detected, the Domme/Dom must pause activities to correct the problem. If the problem is serious, or cannot be corrected, then session activities must be terminated.

22

Contacts

Once established in the role, the Domme/Dom will find it beneficial to be able to exchange ideas and information with other players within the BDSM scene.

There are many formal activities in larger cities around the world, with some centred around particular fetishes such as latex/rubber. Many of the larger bondage parlours host various types of parties, and these are an excellent opportunity for new Dommes/Doms to meet other and more experienced Dommes/Doms.

These are also opportunities for the Domme/Dom to introduce subs to the BDSM party environment. Obviously, mental games can be played by the Domme/Dom by not explaining anything to the sub before arrival at the venue.

These parties are also good for the exchange of ideas, gathering of information, and meeting people and perhaps establishing new friendships within the BDSM scene.

Once the circle of friends (both for Domme/Dom and sub) is established, and growing, it may be fitting for the new Domme/Dom to host a gathering. The gathering may be themed based on a particular fetish.

CONTACTS

These gatherings take substantial planning, and special consideration must be given to the roles and experience of the invited guests. The host will need to schedule some form of entertainment (involving the subs) for the enjoyment of the guests. An extensive example of a dinner party schedule can be found in chapter twenty-nine.

By interacting with participants in the BDSM scene, new Dommes/Doms will gain invaluable knowledge that includes, but is not limited to:

- ✓ Role-play activities
- ✓ BDSM toys
- ✓ BDSM furniture
- ✓ Other people in the BDSM scene
- ✓ Best practices

23

Equipment and Maintenance

For the BDSM enthusiast, there is an overwhelming variety of equipment and clothing for a wide range of role-play scenarios. Some items are easier to source than others.

Purchasing Furniture

Suitable suppliers of BDSM furniture may be difficult to locate. This is another good reason to attend BDSM parties for establishing contacts. There are guidelines below for new Dommes/Doms to follow before making any financial commitment to buying any of these items. These are:
- Decide on the item you need.
- Will it be functional in the preferred or planned role-play scenarios?
- Are there suitable alternatives such as common household items that may be used?
- Although household items may lack the versatility and realism they will suffice while a new scenario is tested.

EQUIPMENT AND MAINTENANCE

Investment into retail BDSM equipment can be made once a scenario has been tried and deemed suitable. As with most other things, the workmanship on the items must be inspected before purchase. Remember that these items may have to undergo severe conditions during role-play. Equipment that cannot take the strain, or that inflicts damage on the role-players, is of little use and dangerous.

Larger furniture items are a significant investment and therefore some level of investigation into alternative sources maybe necessary. For some items the engagement of a suitable tradesperson to custom-build items is a good option. Most tradespeople will be able to construct the furniture, given ample instructions (e.g. the material to be used, the measurements, and the purpose for the furniture). Again, BDSM parties are a great way to gain ideas and make contacts for possible furniture makers in the scene.

Purchasing Clothing

The purchase of clothing largely depends on the role-players and the scenarios that they wish to enact. As with the equipment, consideration must be given to workmanship and to the functionality of the clothing being purchased. The Domme/Dom is faced with decisions on material, colour, size, appearance, ease of cleaning, and the ability to withstand the rigours of roleplay sessions.

For the beginners in the scene, it is recommended to locate local outlets or online stores that sell the equipment and clothing to meet your personal requirements. There may be separate retailers who specialise in leather, rubber/latex products or BDSM equipment. The internet provides easy access to purchasing equipment and clothing from the privacy of your home. Visiting a retail outlet is helpful for determining your size and for trying items before purchasing.

Initially, new players should categorise their requirements as follows:

- ✓ Restraint equipment
- ✓ Punishment equipment
- ✓ Clothing for the Domme/Dom
- ✓ Miscellaneous items

Now, let's look at each group and nominate items to be considered. It is not implied that all these items should be purchased on the first visit to the retailers, but they are items to be considered for purchase.

Restraint equipment

Slave collar: the single most important piece of BDSM equipment. The mere placement of the collar around the sub's neck indicates that role-play has begun. Generally, these collars are made of leather, but they can be metal. Usually they are fitted with a roller buckle but can be styled so that they are locked on the sub using a small padlock. Most collars have 'D' rings for attachments and are often decorated with studs or spikes. Note that when collars are placed on a sub's neck, the Domme/Dom must make sure that it is not too tight by ensuring that two fingers can easily be slid in between the collar and the sub's neck.

EQUIPMENT AND MAINTENANCE

Rope: the most flexible, multi-purpose piece of equipment in any dungeon. Good quality soft rope can be purchased from hardware stores. Buy it in one length, and then cut it to required lengths (short, medium, and long) when back home. Once the rope is cut, the ends of the rope should be bound with electrical tape to prevent fraying. Suitable lengths for the ropes to be cut are two, four, and six metres long.

Chains: not as flexible as rope, they are stronger and create more 'atmosphere'. Depending where the role-play is to take place, the new players may want to use chains. If the role-play is to occur in the bedroom, then spreadeagled in chains is an excellent method of quickly securing the sub to the bed.

Cuffs: for wrists and/or ankles. These may be considered essential, particularly if the role-play is going to take place somewhere other than in the bedroom. Generally, they are made from leather and fitted with roller buckles, can also be metal, and can be fitted with locking devices. An alternative here is to use police-styled hand cuffs and leg cuffs that have inbuilt locking mechanisms. Ropes tied around the ankles and wrists can also be used in place of cuffs.

EQUIPMENT AND MAINTENANCE

Mittens: made from leather. They can be purchased in short style to just cover the hands and wrists, or in long style that lace up to the shoulders. These are very effective in controlling hands and fingers. 'D' ring attachments also are useful for further restraint. Ropes may be used to begin with for restraining hands and wrists.

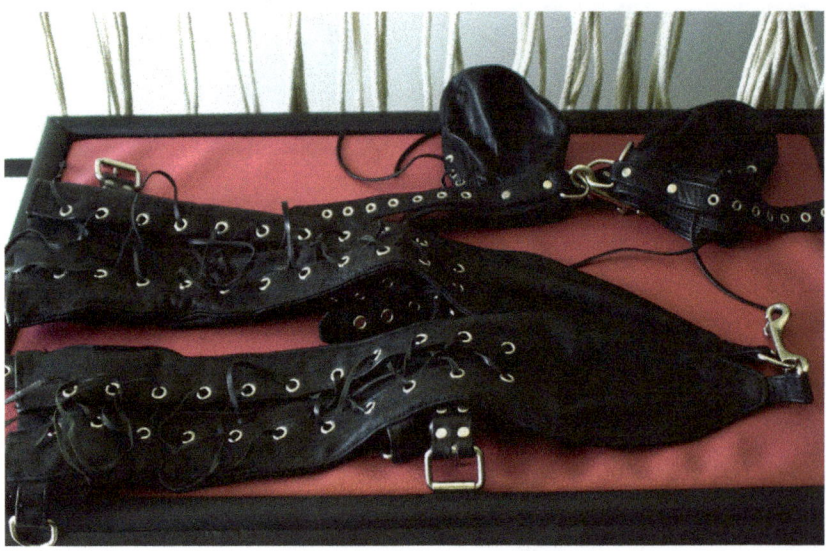

Gags: available in a wide variety of styles, materials, and colours. It is recommended that at least one gag be included in the initial purchase. The type of gag will depend on the personal preferences of the players, and the intended scenario.

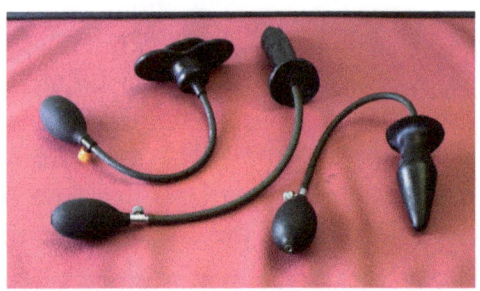

Blindfolds: also available in a wide variety of styles, materials, and colours. Again, it is recommended that at least one blindfold be included in the initial purchase. The type of blindfold will depend on the personal preferences of the players, and the intended scenario.

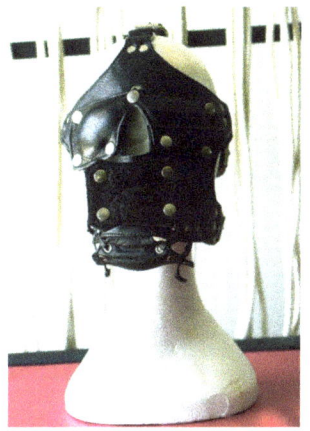

Masks and hoods: available in an endless variety of styles, materials, and colours. Open-faced latex masks are good for beginners because gags and blindfolds can easily be added or removed as required by the Domme/Dom. Intricate facemasks with built-in gags and blindfolds are more restrictive on the sub, but the gags and blindfolds cannot be added or removed without taking the whole mask off the sub. Full-faced latex masks are very restrictive and not recommended for beginners. For full-face coverage, beginners are better to invest in a leather slave hood that has removable gag and blindfold. They are not as tight and restrictive about the sub's face.

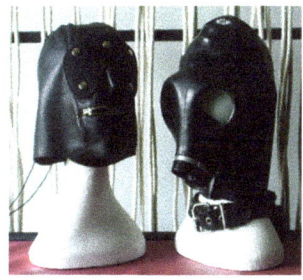

A latex gas mask: These masks are designed for full-face coverage with extreme ease of breathing; however, this can be regulated by the Domme/Dom. Gags and blindfolds can be worn as well, under the gas mask. An interesting touch is to smear a non-toxic body cream on the inside of the lenses of the

EQUIPMENT AND MAINTENANCE

gas mask. This will allow the sub to make out images, but those images will be badly blurred. Once the mask is on, and even if hands are free, the sub can do nothing about the blurred vision.

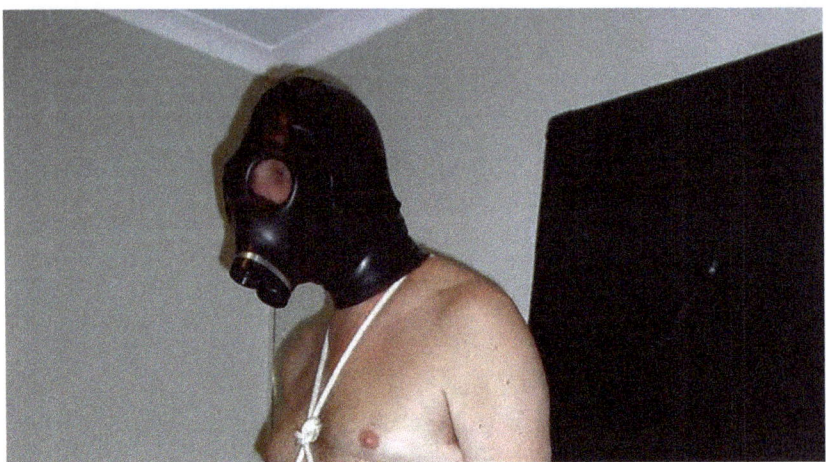

Punishment equipment

Most of the punishment items are self-explanatory, the effect of each item on the body of the sub is unique. The purchase of these items will depend on the effects the Domme/Dom wishes to inflict on the sub. The punishment equipment to be considered at the initial purchase includes but is not limited to:

- ✓ Riding crop
- ✓ Paddle
- ✓ Strap
- ✓ Flogger
- ✓ Thick cane (for bruising effect)
- ✓ Thin cane (for stinging effect)
- ✓ Nipple clamps

BOUND FOR PLAY - BDSM TRAINING MANUAL

Riding Crops

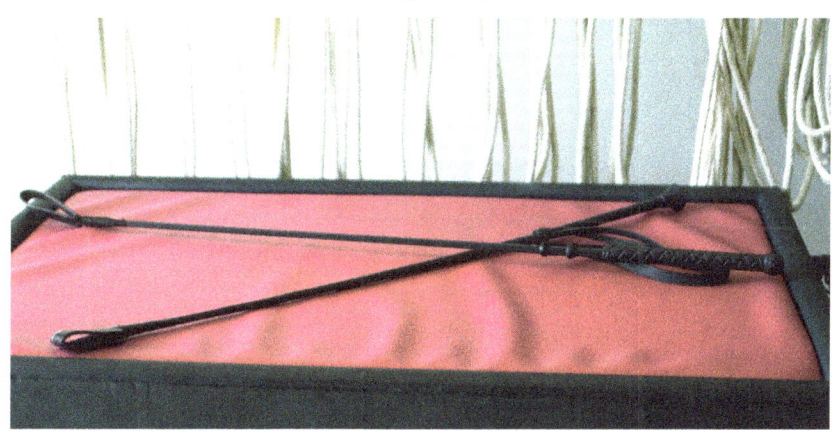

Paddles

Cat 'o' nine tails

Nipple clamps

Clothing for the Domme/Dom

Clothing particularly for the female Domme, is available in an endless array of styles and colours. Preferred materials for the clothing are leather, latex, and PVC. Appropriate boots and/or shoes should be considered (i.e. stiletto heels, 6"/15cm and patent leather (as boot/shoe/foot worship is a popular fetish). Leather or PVC gloves (long and/or short) are also an important addition.

PVC

EQUIPMENT AND MAINTENANCE

Leather

Latex

Miscellaneous items

There are several miscellaneous items that MUST be available to all BDSM role-players. These items include:

- ✓ Latex surgical gloves for use during anal play
- ✓ Antiseptics/disinfectants for cleaning furniture and equipment
- ✓ Towels for personal use
- ✓ Condoms for use on insertable equipment and for use with any sexual activity
- ✓ Safety knife or scissors for quick release from rope bondage
- ✓ Candles for atmosphere lighting and for hot wax sessions
- ✓ Enema for use prior to anal sessions

Maintenance of Equipment

Now that the new role-players have made their initial investment and purchased their first bundle of 'toys' for their BDSM games, they need to be aware of the necessary maintenance of the equipment. Proper maintenance of equipment is habit-forming, and it is a good habit. Like most other assets in life, if equipment is maintained correctly, it will allow longer and more reliable service.

Where possible, have equipment hanging up when not in use. Preferably, have designated places for all pieces of equipment, and try to avoid leaving them lying on the floor when not in use. To pack them away, use a chest of drawers, a cupboard, or a wardrobe.

When equipment is used during a session, and when that usage is finished, do not replace it in its normal storage position. Leave it lying on the floor. It becomes obvious then that equipment lying

EQUIPMENT AND MAINTENANCE

on the floor has been used during a session and it requires cleaning before being returned to its normal storage place.

Most items (including ropes) are easily cleaned by wiping with a soft cloth and with some disinfectant or antiseptic solution on them. However, all latex apparel must be washed in warm soapy water and hung out to dry, most likely in a shower recess. Avoid leaving the latex in direct sunlight as this will cause the latex to deteriorate.

Ropes should be stored hanging from a rail so that the Domme/Dom has easy access during session to all ropes knowing that they are free of knots and tangles. Similarly, chains must be stored in a manner that keeps them free of tangling. Any furniture used during the session also needs to be cleaned, including the floor.

24

Courtesy

Points of courtesy will vary according to the requirements of the players depending on their environments. However, BDSM courtesies should be extended across the entire BDSM world. Players should be treated according to their roles in the scene once the respective roles have been identified and accepted.

COURTESY

This applies to BDSM parties, internet chat, emails, telephone conversations, and face-to-face encounters. This is particularly important when players from the opposite side of a D/s relations are communicating, and if two Dommes/Doms are communicating with each other in the presence of subs.

25

Etiquette

Points of etiquette also will vary according to the requirements of the players and their intended environments. However, there are accepted BDSM behaviours, particularly for subs. It is recommended that the Domme/Dom details the expected behaviour from a sub at the beginning of the D/s relationship. Some examples may be, never look Mistress in the eye, never speak without asking for permission first, always thank your Domme/Dom for punishments given. Obviously, in a long-term relationship, these will need to be amended as the activities within the relationship change such as asking permission to use the bathroom (applies for maids and subs not restrained).

Etiquette for a sub in a role-play scenario encompasses many of the details already discussed in previous chapters, such as body language, appearance, and physical activities.

26

Acceptance of Roles

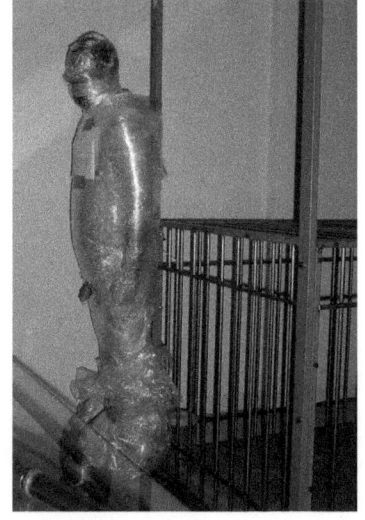

Dommes/Doms are responsible for the wellbeing of their subs during BDSM role-play scenarios. Dommes/Doms **MUST** accept this responsibility; otherwise there will not be trust from the sub in the ability and intentions of the Domme/Dom.

Subs will enter a D/s relationship only when that **trust** in the Domme/Dom has been established. A sub is more likely to develop the **trust** in the Domme/Dom if the Domme/Dom has discussed all the aspects detailed in the early chapters of this manual prior to entering any role-play scenario, including the checklist.

In the case of long-term D/s relationships, the acceptance of roles will be documented and supported by the slavery agreement. An example is attached at the end of this manual.

27

Guide to roleplay

Are you ready? Let's go!
By following the instructions of this manual and checking the step-by-step action plan below, the players will be able to reach a level of confidence and competence for role play scenarios in a very short time. They will have the satisfaction of knowing that they have covered all the critical aspects such as **health, hygiene, safety, consent** and personal **limits** of the players.

Having reached this stage, they will continue to develop as they gain more experience and as they expand their network of friends within the BDSM world. Because of their understanding of the various activities, the people involved, and the associated etiquette, they will be readily accepted by other BDSM players. As with all social arenas, there will be those that they wish to avoid, but others where a close friendship will be established.

Here is a step-by-step action plan for novice role-players.

1. **Communication:**
   When individuals have decided they wish to become

involved with BDSM, or they would like to experiment, they need to communicate their feelings with their partners.

2. **Consent:**
Both partners need to consent to proceed with any involvement or experiments. Covered in detail in chapter ten. Note that consent may be given in stages, to be reviewed after particular activities, and before proceeding to the next phase of involvement.

3. **Trust:**
Before consent is given by the partners, there must be at least a small element of trust between them. From this point onwards, the trust between the partners will grow and ultimately will strengthen the overall relationship.

4. **Planning the initial session:**
The role-players need to take the time to plan the activities of their initial scenario based on the checklist. This scenario should take no more than a total of one hour.

5. **Roles for the initial session:**
For both novice players to be able to fully evaluate the initial session, it will be necessary to switch roles. They need to decide who will take which role first. The switching should occur approximately mid way through the one-hour session.

6. **Identifying the household items to use:**
As part of their planning, the players need to identify

which standard household items they will be using in the initial session, as it is highly unlikely they will have specialised BDSM equipment. Not only has the equipment to be identified, also the way it is going to be used in the session needs to be carefully planned. This is a critical phase of the session planning.

7. **Safe word:**
   A safe word (or action) must be identified for use by the players for times when the sub experiences difficulties and needs to be released from a particular position. It is advisable that once a safe word is established, that this same word be kept for use in all future sessions. Bear in mind the traffic light system explained in chapter eight.

8. **Evaluation of initial session:**
   At the end of the initial session, the players must put forward their personal assessment of the session. They should discuss both the good and bad aspects of the session and both roles they played, plus the equipment used, and the scenarios that were played out by each of them. They need to decide whether to continue with BDSM role-playing in future, or not. If one or either of the partners elects not to proceed, then this constitutes a withdrawal of consent.

9. **Repeat sessions:**
   If both partners consent to continue with role-play after the initial session, then follow up sessions should be used to explore their desire to progress into the BDSM world. After each session, an evaluation and discussion are required to ensure that each partner is

committed, emotionally and financially in continuing BDSM role-playing sessions.

10. Roles:
Following the experimental sessions with makeshift equipment, the preferred roles for the players will begin to emerge. Typically, one partner will become more dominant, while the other becomes more submissive. It is also acceptable to maintain role switching as their involvement in BDSM continues.

11. Acceptance of roles:
Once the roles have been allocated to the partners, they must accept the responsibility that those roles imply.

12. Relationship:
The D/s relationship between the players needs to be established. For most newcomers to the BDSM scene, this relationship will be a casual affair, on an as required (or desired) basis. A good alternative is to set aside a fixed time on a regular basis.

13. Safety:
Although the safe word had already been in use, this needs to be re-affirmed by the players before each session begins. Also, the use of drugs and alcohol prior to, and during, the session is not recommended.

14. Hygiene:
If the partners have been together for some time, it is not likely that they would need to undergo a health check to detect any communicable diseases. If the partners are new to each other, this is a recommended

precaution. Hygiene standards for the room, equipment, and clothing must be maintained at a high level, with both players being conscious of hygiene at all times.

15. Checklist:
The Dominant partner must prepare a checklist of BDSM activities for the submissive partner to fill out. This exercise may be repeated at a future date once the sub has had more experience and may wish to change some of the responses on the checklist. The sub is encouraged to respond to all questions on the list. The Domme/Dom will then be able to use the list to assist in the planning of various role-play scenarios.

16. Limits:
Both players should define their personal limits. They must respect the limits defined by the other player. Note that limits most likely will change after various scenarios have been experienced. These changes should be noted on the sub's checklist, or a new checklist drawn up.

17. Agreement:
In the case of a 24/7 full time relationship, a detailed slavery agreement needs to be drawn up and signed by both players. An example of a slave agreement is attached at the end of this manual.

18. Investment:
The partners need to agree to the level of investment in equipment, clothing and the relationship prior to any session.

GUIDE TO ROLEPLAY

Once these steps have been completed, the players are ready for role-playing scenarios.

NOTE - Many players 'short cut' these preparations in their eagerness to get involved in role-play. Invariably, they will have to address the aspects they bypassed, or they become issues that need to be resolved. If they don't, then they are playing in scenarios that are not as safe, hygienic, or as satisfying as they should be. Following these steps will lead new BDSM enthusiasts safely and confidently into the highly enjoyable and satisfying realm of BDSM role-playing.

28

Specific Activities

Specific Activity No. 1: Tying a Triple Loop and Cinch

The most basic requirement for using ropes is being able to secure the sub with a quick, easy, and effective knot. The recommended procedure is to use a triple loop and cinch binding. This is most useful for binding together the sub's wrists, elbows, ankles, knees, and/or thighs. In this example, a sub's wrists will be bound together using the triple loop and cinch.

To begin, select a length of rope and fold in half, to use the recommended double rope bondage technique. The rope will now have a loop (being the centre of the length of rope) at one extremity, with the two loose ends at the other extremity.

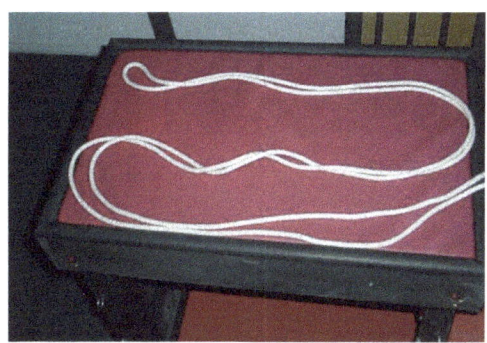

SPECIFIC ACTIVITIES

Take the looped end of the rope and pass the length of the rope around the wrists and then through the loop. This gives the first loop around the wrists.

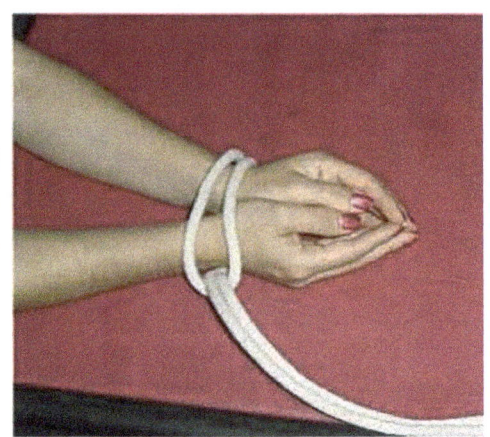

Pull the length of rope back in the opposite direction so that the first loop becomes snug, but not tight. Moving in the same direction, wrap the length of rope around the wrists twice more, thus giving the second and third loops.

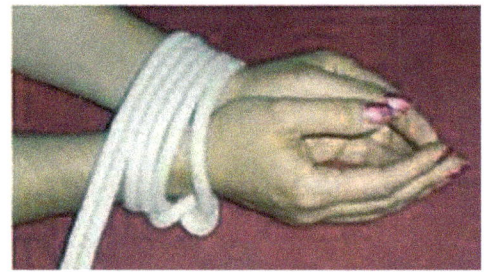

In the same direction, then pass the ropes around one wrist only. The ropes should then be brought forward to fit between the hands.

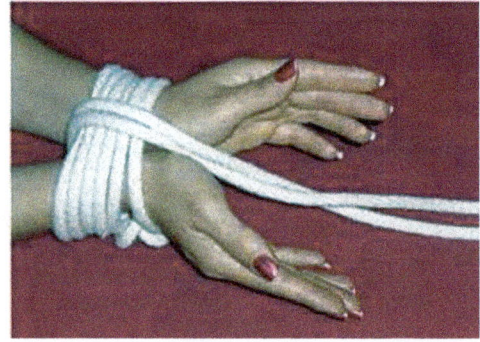

Take the lengths of rope and pass them back between and under the triple loop, bring back to the top, then pull the ropes forward snugly. This is the cinch and will tighten the triple loop around the sub's wrists. Pass a single rope length under a single strand of the triple loop at the front of the wrists. This will provide a tie-off point.

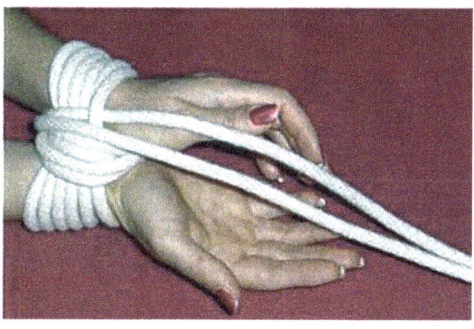

Tie off with a double wreath knot, then attach the loose ends of the rope to any fixture, making sure that the sub's fingers cannot reach that fixture.

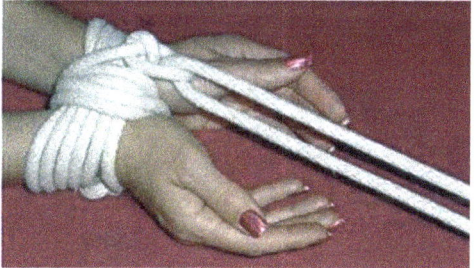

With just a little practice, this procedure will become second nature to Dommes/Doms. It is a quick and effective way to restrain a sub's limbs, working equally as well for wrists, elbows, ankles, knees, and thighs. Remember to have the knot facing away from palms of hands.

Specific Activity No. Two: Tying a Rope Body Harness

A rope body harness is deceivingly constrictive. When done correctly, it will look very impressive and place the sub in tight bondage through a process that steadily increases the pressure on the body of the sub. Once the harness is complete, then the

SPECIFIC ACTIVITIES

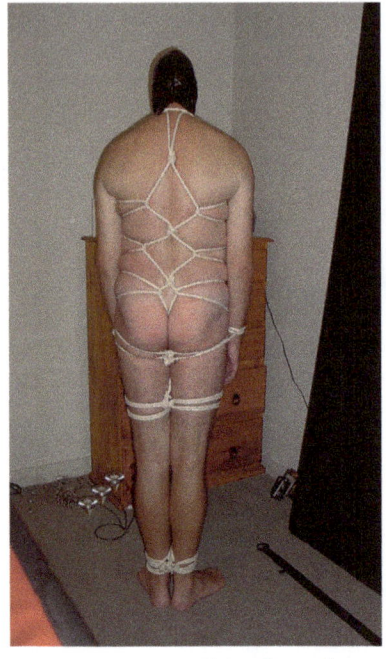

Domme/Dom is free to engage in other activities to derive pleasure from the sub.

As with most of the rope work in BDSM, it is recommended that the 'double rope bondage' system be used when applying a rope harness. Double rope bondage is started by taking the two ends of the length of rope in one hand, and then pulling the rope through the hand until the loop (being the centre of the rope) has been reached. This loop (the halfway point of the rope) is used as the

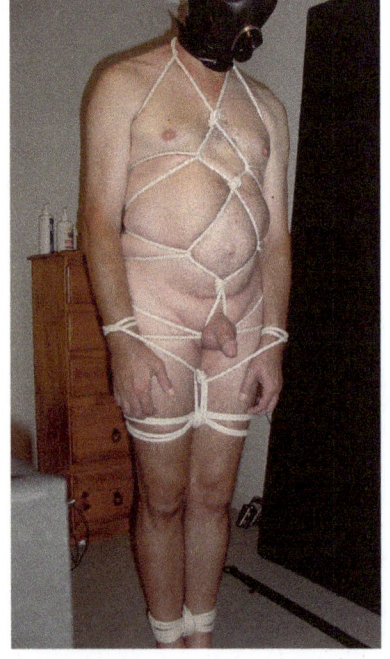

starting point for the placement of rope(s) on the sub. The effects of double rope bondage become apparent once the harness is progressed.

For the rope body harness, choose a length of rope approximately six metres in length, therefore, working in double three metre lengths. The sub should be standing, legs slightly apart and arms slightly akimbo.

Begin by placing the centre of the rope (the loop) at the back of the sub's neck and then bring both strands of rope around the neck to meet high on the sub's chest. Tie the ropes together using a simple wreath knot. Note that although the reference indicates more than one rope, it is actually the single rope extending from the central loop point (now at the back of the sub's neck). There is no need for complicated knots here as the simplistic wreath knot is quite enough.

It is important to note that whenever knots are tied on the harness that the bulk of each knot must be facing **outwards**, and not pressing into the body of the sub. As the harness becomes tighter, and if the knots are inwards facing, then severe discomfort and possible internal injury could be caused to the sub. The sub will experience enough discomfort without having to suffer the bruising effects of incorrectly tied knots.

The ropes should now be hanging loosely down the front of the sub's torso. Tie the next knot between the breasts, with a third knot tied just below the breasts, and a fourth knot just above the genital area.

At this point, if a vaginal plug and/or butt plug is to be used, it should be inserted before any further harness tying is done. Once any required plugs are safely in the sub's openings, then the ropes may be passed between the legs and up the back, thus holding the plugs in place. Note that the sub may have to assist here with the plugs until the ropes are drawn tautly enough to be able to maintain the plugs in their desired positions.

Alternatively, if plugs are not being used, the Domme/Dom may wish to draw the ropes towards the hips, thus allowing easy access later to the vaginal and/or anal areas. This option will be discussed as the tying of the harness progresses.

With the double ropes running up the centre of the sub's back, knots should be tied to correspond with the knots at the front of the sub. In other words, the knots should occur at the same distance from the shoulders, front and back.

When the ropes reach the shoulders of the sub, pass the ropes

SPECIFIC ACTIVITIES

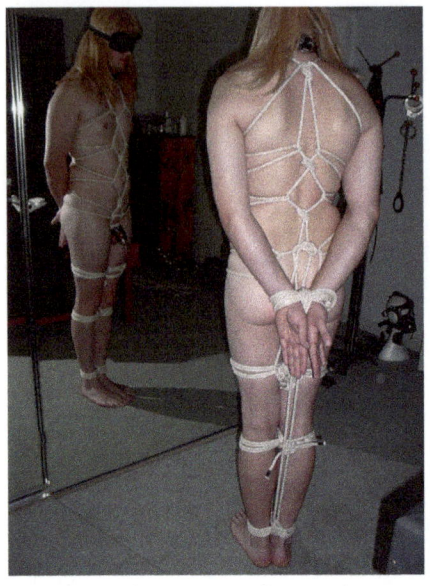

under the rope around the back of the sub's neck. Pull the ropes downwards, and back towards the sub's shoulder blades. This will have two effects. It will tighten the ropes under the sub's crotch, and it will draw the rope away from the back of the neck, thus placing the strain on the shoulders, and not the neck.

Pass each of the ropes under an arm and then loop around a single strand of the knotted ropes running down the centre of the sub's chest. Loop around a strand of the central rope between the first and second knots. Pull each of the ropes back to each side of the sub, around the back, loop around the central ropes again, and then back to the front, this time between the second and third knots. There now should be ropes crossing from centre to side of the sub both above and below the breasts, as well as the knot in between the breasts. For female subs, the positions of these ropes will serve as anchor points for more detailed breast bondage. Breast bondage should be applied separately to the rope harness, and after the rope harness has been completed.

Note that each time the central ropes (front and back) are pulled to the side of the sub's torso they form diamond patterns and they become progressively tighter on the sub.

Continue this method of intertwining the rope strands with the central ropes at the front and back of the sub until the genital area is reached. As the ropes here are pulled outwards (and tightened) the genital area will be freed, ready to receive specialised attention after the harness is completed. However, if a vaginal and/or butt plug is being used, the ropes passing under the torso must be left in position and could even be re-enforced by passing the ropes through again.

Now, the main body of the harness is complete. If the ropes have been kept taut at each connection between front-side-back, then the harness will, by now, be very restricting on the sub. Note to keep checking the condition of the sub, paying particular attention for any problems with cramping, circulation, and breathing. Keep talking (threatening, if in roleplay) the sub to monitor their condition.

Depending on the length of rope being used, and the size of the sub being harnessed, there may be considerable length of rope left unused, hanging from the sub. If there is enough rope, extend the bondage downwards to include the thighs, knees, and ankles.

As the ropes extend down, tie a knot above the knees. Then, bind the ropes three times around the legs at that point and above the knot. Then pass the ropes between the legs and around the ropes that have just been placed around the legs. Do this twice and finish off by tying to the knot originally tied above the knees. Repeat this process below the knees, and again at the ankles (rope permitting).

Again, remain particularly aware of the sub's condition.

Once the main harness is completed, additional ropes may be used to restrict arms and wrists. And, of course, separate ropes may be used to apply various forms of breast bondage on female subs.

Remember to have a safety knife close at hand. If the sub experiences difficulties and requires immediate release, it is easier to cut the ropes rather than spending time trying to untie all the knots.

Also, when releasing the sub from the ropes, be particularly careful to prevent rope burns. These burns are caused simply by dragging the ropes over the skin. It is painful (not a problem), breaks the skin and can cause infection (which is a problem), and can generate the burn marks that may last for a very long time (a problem). To avoid burns, the Domme/Dom should place fingers between the ropes and the sub's skin when drawing ropes across the sub's body.

SPECIFIC ACTIVITIES

Specific Activity No. Three: Performing a Hog Tie

A hog tie is a very punishing position for a sub. The sub needs to be fit and healthy as this position puts strain on the chest, stomach, arms, and legs. This must not be used on subs that have breathing difficulties, arthritis and joint pain or circulation problems in the limbs. Preferably, the sub should be lying on a soft surface to help relieve the pressure on chest and stomach.

It is also advisable that if the sub is wearing a slave collar (as she/he should be), then that collar may need to be loosened or removed altogether while the sub is in the hog tie position. Otherwise, unnecessary pressure may be placed on the throat. A good idea is to confirm a safe word before sub is placed in a hogtie position. This is important in case sub gets cramping or pain during the bondage. The safe word should be different from the one that puts a complete halt to the session. This is so Domme/Dom can untie sub, and both still remain in role-play. The red and orange light system can also be used here.

If ropes are being used to bind ankles and wrists, then the standard triple loop and cinch method should be used. Alternatively, it is equally effective to use arm or wrist binders with ankle binders.

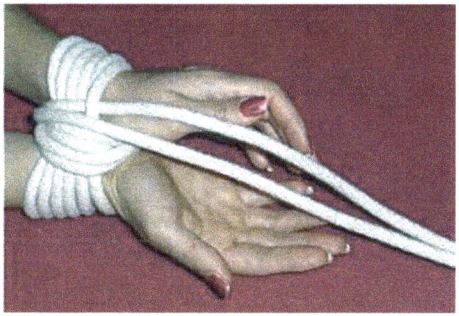

Start the position by the sub lying face down, with slave collar either loosened or removed. Secure the wrists behind the back, using either rope or leather wrist cuffs. Full leather arm binders or leather mittens (either short or long) can be effective alternatives. It is the Domme's/Dom's choice regarding the use of restraints.

Secure the ankles using either rope or leather ankle cuffs. An alternative here is that a leg spreader bar may also be used so that the legs are splayed instead of being pressed together.

Then, using rope, tie the bound ankles to the bound wrists. The ankles do not have to be touching the wrists. The closer they are drawn together by the rope, the more the discomfort for the sub.

If the feet are exposed, then the Domme/Dom has an opportunity to apply interesting forms of discipline to the soles of the sub's feet. The Domme/Dom can use a huge range of items here, ranging from feathers and ice cubes to crops and canes.

SPECIFIC ACTIVITIES

The Domme/Dom needs to be constantly aware of the sub's condition and any problems as soon as they arise, as with all bondage positions. For subs with knee and joint pain or any other health issues, this position is not recommended.

Specific Activity No. Four: Conducting a Full Spanking Session

Spanking is probably one of the most common activities in BDSM role-play. Consequently, there are numerous variations to positions, roles, and toys used.

Basically, there are two approaches to spanking. The first is to use the more severe implements immediately. These implements would include crops, canes, and whips. This method has maximum impact on the sub, but the duration of the session will be curtailed, depending on the sub's ability to absorb the pain.

The second method uses an approach generally known as a 'warm up'. This method allows the Domme/Dom to gradually increase the intensity of the punishment and may even include short relief breaks. Eventually, the Domme/Dom will use the most severe implements, but because of the gradual build up, the sub is much more likely to be able to endure the punishment for a longer time. It is this second method that will be analysed in the following paragraphs.

For a serious spanking session, the sub needs to be bound securely. This does not mean that the bonds need to be tight, but the sub must be immobilised. This may be achieved by using ankle and wrist cuffs, secured by ropes, leather straps, and/or chains. There are several items of bondage furniture that are suitable for spanking sessions, and these can be used, restricting the sub into the desired position. For players without this furniture, chairs, lounge or a sturdy coffee table are good for forcing the sub into a position for spanking.

It is possible for the sub to remain standing to receive punishment, but as the target area for spanking generally is the buttocks, and if the sub is standing, then there is a danger of misdirected blows striking the sub high above the buttocks thus causing damage to the kidney area.

The most suitable spanking position is to have the sub bent forward so that the exposed buttocks are kept taut, ready to receive maximum impact of the punishment.

Further preparation of the sub should include a gag to muffle the screams of enjoyment, earplugs as a surprise of various implements being used when least expected, as well as a blindfold to prevent the sub suffering from information overload about activities in the session.

Once the sub is securely immobilised in a suitably exposed position where gag, ear plugs, and blindfold are in place, then all is ready.

SPECIFIC ACTIVITIES

The warm up should begin with the Domme/Dom using a hand smacking into the target area. Some sharp blows evenly distributed across the buttock area will start to get the sub's blood circulating. The type of blows can be varied by the Domme/Dom slightly cupping the hand and then hitting the target area rapidly with upwards and downwards movements of the wrist. This process can continue until the Domme/Dom tires of delivering the blows (change hands if hand gets sore). The timing between the blows can be varied. Whilst it may be good for the Domme/Dom to get into an even rhythm, it is better to keep the sub waiting for the next strike, not knowing when it will arrive, nor if there will be a change of implement being used.

Next to be used is the light flogger (note; images of the following equipment in chapter twenty-three).

This can be used with forceful blows across the target area, and it can also be used on the upper back, the backs of the legs and particularly on the soles of the feet (if they are exposed for the attention of the Domme/Dom). Note that when punishing the bottoms of the feet, only the soles of the feet should be struck, and not the instep area. The flogger provides a warm tingling sensation (not quite a sting) for the recipient to enjoy. This can be used at the Domme's/Dom's pleasure, ensuring even treatment over the selected target areas.

Next to be used is the paddle. They look very much like table tennis bats, and sometimes have patterns cut out of them, and this causes a patterned effect on the target area (to amuse the Domme/Dom, no doubt). The paddle delivers a heavy, dull thud into the target area, and it should only be used on the buttocks. It is recommended that the paddle be used sparingly (at discretion of the Domme/Dom, of course) because of the thudding effect on the sub.

At the discretion of the Domme/Dom, some relief may be administered to the sub. It is good to rub talcum powder onto the reddened target area. When the powder is gently rubbed onto the skin, it has an extremely smooth and calming effect on the sub. This is a wonderful preparation for the increasing intensity of the punishment that is to follow.

The next toys to be used are straps. As the name implies a strap is simply a piece of broad, flat leather, attached to a handle. For that little bit extra effect, use a double strap, where there are two strips of leather attached to the handle. When striking the target area, straps emit a loud smacking sound, which is very comforting for the Domme/Dom to hear after the negligible response sounds from hands, floggers, and paddles. A loud smacking noise from a strap indicates to the Domme/Dom that the blows are landing hard and true. The sub will be enjoying the lift in intensity of the blows, knowing that the Domme/Dom has total control and is moving, inevitably, towards the heavier punishment. If the Domme/Dom wishes, more talcum powder can be applied during or after the strapping process (it is amusing to watch the powder fly as leather strikes reddened skin). Straps can be used on the soles (not insteps) of the sub's feet.

Following the strap(s), the next item to be used on the sub is the riding crop. This is a smaller strap but attached to a longer and more flexible handle. The crop will sting the sub, and Dommes/Doms can amuse themselves by leaving crop patterns across the target area on the sub. The intensity of the blows is at the discretion of the Domme/Dom. Crops can be used on the soles (not insteps) of the sub's feet.

By now, the target area should be glowing crimson red with a multitude of patterns all over it. If this is not the case, then the Domme/Dom must go back to repeat some of the punishments as the preparation has been incomplete and has not produced the required result.

Next to be used is the cane, and this session is now moving into the heavier disciplines, sometimes referred to as 'corporal punishment'. From now until the end of the session, the Domme/

SPECIFIC ACTIVITIES

Dom really needs to be aware of how far the sub can be pushed with this type of punishment. They must remain extremely vigilant in monitoring the condition of the sub. Two types of canes can be used, either thick or thin, but both must be freely flexible in the hand. A thin cane will tend to cut the skin and have a burning stinging effect on the sub, while a thick cane will bruise the target area (while still stinging the sub) and will tend to leave longer lasting marks on the sub.

One interesting stroke to use with the cane is to bring it down very hard in a vertical swing, just barely brushing the exposed buttocks of the sub. When done correctly, this produces an incredible but brief burning sting. This generally takes the sub by surprise when blows of lesser intensity are expected to be delivered square onto the buttocks. This is a nice variation for a Domme/Dom to employ.

The objectives of the Domme/Dom here (apart from personal enjoyment) are to take the sub to, or beyond, the sub's limits. Also, of importance is the delivery of the blows from the cane. Ideally, an equal number of strokes (and therefore stripes) should be delivered to each buttock of the sub. It is good if the stripes are parallel and even better if they are grouped very close together. Of course, crossing stripes are permissible. The result will be a work of art by the Domme/Dom, and no one can be proud of sloppy art work. This most probably will require repeated sessions to attain a respectable conclusion. No doubt the sub will delight in providing the canvas for this artistry!

An interesting variation here in between strokes, is to cool down the sub's target area with ice. This will have a startling effect on the sub at first, and then will begin to sooth the inflamed areas. However, when the caning resumes, the intensity of the pain inflicted will intensify because of the application of ice to the target area.

However, there is one more step to complete this session, and that is the use of the whip. In this scenario, a cat-o-nine tails will be used. Because of the severity of the 'cat', it is advised to only use this if the sub has previously agreed to it or has agreed to allow the Domme/Dom to push the limits further than previously. Here, the Domme/Dom must remain particularly aware of the sub's condition and must be prepared for the sub to use the safe word or pre-defined traffic light safety signal.

Once the session has completed, the Domme/Dom may leave the sub (under constant surveillance, of course) in the bound position to recover. While this is happening, the Domme/Dom may amuse Herself/Himself by making patterns on the sub's back using hot wax. This tingling, burning sensation can be relaxing for a sub who is recovering from a session of the whip or cane.

Remember that the Domme/Dom can stop the spanking process at any level desired within the limitations of the sub. Also, the intensity of the session is entirely at the discretion of the Domme/Dom (e.g. the cane and cat may be used, but only lightly, or, the soles of the feet must not be hit at all).

Spanking sessions are a basic scenario for most BDSM couples. There are so many variables in these sessions that they can be tailored to suit the participants. The variables are the individual pieces of equipment and furniture to be used, the position to be used by the sub, the length of time each piece of equipment is used, and the intensity of the blows from each piece of equipment.

Specific Activity No. Five: Effective Mummification

Mummification is enjoyed by those who have a fetish for total immobilisation for long periods of time, and on occasions, it is coupled with a breath control fetish. For this activity, mummification will be described without breath control, meaning that adequate breathing will be available to the sub at all times.

The attraction is the absolute immobilisation. Generally, this is not an uncomfortable position for the sub, and therefore it can

SPECIFIC ACTIVITIES

be endured for long periods of time. The sub can be mummified in either the standing or laying positions. For scenarios where the female is Domme and the male is sub, it should be remembered that moving a mummified sub can be quite a heavy task (depending on the physique of the role-players). Therefore, it is a good idea to make sure that the sub is in the right location/position before the mummification process begins.

Of course, the Domme/Dom can make some adjustments to the sub before the process begins so that the sub gets the maximum enjoyment from the session. Some of these adjustments may include;
- butt plug (vibrating)
- vaginal plug (for female mummies, and vibrating preferred)
- cock and ball bondage (for male mummies)

- nipple clamps
- earplugs
- gag fitted with a breathing tube

It is recommended a blindfold always be used on the sub to prevent damage to the eyes when the wrapping material is removed.

CAUTION:
In the case of subs that have asthma or breathing difficulties and would still like to experience this scenario, it is strongly advised, not to wrap the head of the sub. A leather or open faced latex hood should be used over the head. If any difficulties arise, it is quicker and safer to remove the hood than cutting the wrap. The sub can still experience hours of pleasure, at the discretion of the Domme/Dom without any risk to their health and safety.

The material most commonly used for mummification is known as pallet wrap, used commercially to wrap around products contained on wooden pallets. In effect, this is very similar to the plastic wrap commonly used in kitchens to keep food fresh or to use as a food cover in microwave ovens. Pallet wrap can be purchased in large rolls. Although clear wrap is the most popular, it can also be purchased in black or various other colours. As with all other bondage, the Domme/Dom needs to consider what needs to be done if the sub has to be released from bondage quickly. Consequently, a reliable safety knife or scissors need to be at the Domme's/Dom's disposal. Obviously, extreme care must be taken when releasing the sub using the knife.

Once the sub is in position and the various pieces of equipment are in place, the Domme/Dom is ready to begin. The process of being wrapped in plastic will cause the sub to perspire, some more freely than others. This means the Domme/Dom needs to consider protective material such as towels or sheeting under the sub to prevent damage to floor coverings when the wrap is cut

SPECIFIC ACTIVITIES

away. Secondly, if it is planned to leave the sub mummified for an extended period (e.g. more than two hours), then the Domme/Dom must provide water (through a straw) for the mummified sub. The Domme/Dom may decide to leave the sub in this position for several hours. If this is the plan, then the Domme/Dom must decide beforehand if the sub is permitted to use the bathroom before the process begins. If the Domme/Dom denies the sub this right, then the Domme/Dom must be prepared for additional moisture when the wrap is cut away. This indeed may be deliberately planned by the Domme/Dom, and promoted by administering large quantities of water to the mummified sub.

So now, the mummification process can begin.

Begin by wrapping plastic around one hand and instruct the sub to make a fist once the wrap has been passed around the hand. Wrap the plastic around the fist. This process effectively seals off the loose opening around the fingers. Gradually wind the wrap up to the armpit, and then wind back down to the wrist again. Tear the plastic off the roll at this point. There now should be a double layer of plastic wrap encasing the first arm. Note that the wrap should not be too tight because it is not the intention to restrict the blood flow through the body and limbs.

Repeat the process for the second arm.

Next, instruct the sub to lift one foot. Begin by wrapping around the foot, and once the foot is back in the original position, gradually wind the wrap all the way up to the crotch. As with the arms, then wind the wrap back down to the foot, then tear the plastic away from the large roll.

Repeat the process for the second leg.

The Domme/Dom should press the plastic wrap on the sub's arms and legs so that it adheres to itself and the sub's skin. Now instruct the sub to move arms and legs into the preferred position. The legs need to be pressed together; however, the Domme/Dom may decide to have the arms positioned at the side, behind, in front, or with hands placed on head or back of neck, or arms folded in front or behind. It is recommended that the arms be left at the subs side, as this position will give the least problems with circulation, and it will make the wrapping process easier.

For subs who want their head wrapped, begin wrapping the head from the top loosely throughout the process to winding down to the neck, remembering to leave an opening at the lips for breathing and drinking. Read the caution at start of this chapter.

Wrap the torso so that the arms are tightly pinned to the body and continue down below the waistline. The nipples and genital areas may be left open if the Domme/Dom wishes to play games with the mummy once wrapping is complete, otherwise, these areas should be securely wrapped as well.

Continue down the legs, wrapping both legs tightly together.

The wrapping from the head down to the ankles should have a minimum of two layers of wrap, at the discretion of the Domme/Dom. It is also possible to wrap the mummy to a piece of furniture, to prevent the mummy from losing balance and falling over (it can be awkward to bring to an upright position again).

When the wrapping is complete, check that the sub still has adequate breathing ability, and give the sub a drink of water through a straw. Water should be supplied on a regular basis to prevent dehydration caused by the plastic wrap. **REMINDER: alcohol should not to be consumed before or during any session by Dommes/Doms and subs. It will impair judgment in this roleplay and may cause serious injury or death to the sub.**

When the time comes for the sub to be released from the wrap, a knife or scissors will have to be used to cut through the layers of plastic. Obvious precautions need to be taken here so that the sub is not injured with the knife. Also, remember that there will be considerable moisture in the wrap from perspiration of the sub, and

SPECIFIC ACTIVITIES

there will be even more if the sub was forced to urinate while still wrapped. (See start of this chapter for moisture control)

Specific Activity No. Six: Complete Cross Dressing

Once again, this is a fetish activity for some men, and it may take various forms of clothing and role-play.

The cross-dressing scenario can be run simultaneously with other BDSM activities. They are discussed further in specific activities in chapter twenty-eight and the dinner party scenario.

As well as deciding in which other activities the cross-dressed sub will be involved, the Domme/Dom will also need to decide if there is to be an overall theme for this role-play session (e.g. dressed as a maid then domestic duties, or dressed as a school girl then discipline, or dressed as a whore then anal sex).

Throughout this type of session there will be an overriding sensation of personal humiliation for the sub. The Domme/Dom can use verbal abuse to keep reminding the sub that he is never good enough and can never measure up to female standards. This becomes a mental torture for the sub and adds to the overwhelming sense of humiliation.

Uniforms or outfits may be purchased for particular themes; otherwise the sub will wear street clothes, ordered to fit.

For the dressing process, the Domme/Dom must ensure that all items of clothing and makeup are readily available for the session. Short cuts or missing items of clothing or makeup will have a disappointing effect on the sub, so it is worth the effort to check before the session begins that everything is available. Also, if required by the Domme/Dom, the sub's nails should be painted prior to the session.

As each tedious step is performed, the mental awareness of the transformation is impressed on the sub. Unless the sub needs help getting dressed, the Domme/Dom should watch very closely every movement of the struggling sub, usually making derogatory comments to make sure that he never forgets his role, and his embarrassment.

The sub should completely undress and present himself to his Mistress. The slave collar must be the first thing a Domme/Dom places around their slave's neck. This signifies ownership of that slave and the roleplay has begun. At this point, the Domme/Dom may decide to use cock and ball bondage, this is optional. The first items of clothing, obviously, will be the underwear, panties and bra. As the man will have no boobs to fill the bra (usually) then it will need to be artificially filled. Rubber inserts can be purchased, but it is just as easy to use paper or old stockings.

Next, put on stockings, not pantyhose. Use the stay up variety of stocking, unless it is planned that the sub will be wearing suspenders. In that case, next on is the suspender belt, then clip up stockings.

Now it's time for the outer clothing, be that dress, or uniform, or skirt and top.

SPECIFIC ACTIVITIES

Next come the shoes. These will need to be the correct fitting for the sub. And, in theme with the feminisation of the sub, the heels will need to be high, at least 5"- 6",(12-15cm). It is advisable to avoid stiletto heels as the chunkier style of heel is more suitable to support the weight of the sub.

Now for the facial makeup. It helps if the sub has shaved closely before the session, however the Domme/Dom may have to work around moustaches and beards. The Domme/Dom will have to apply the makeup, although once the sub goes through repeated sessions of this nature, perhaps part of the training will be learning to apply makeup himself. This can then be used as a means of determining punishment for the little 'sissy'. Makeup should not be spared. Use makeup base, blush, powders, lipstick, lip liner, eyeliner, eye shadow, mascara or false stick-on lashes.

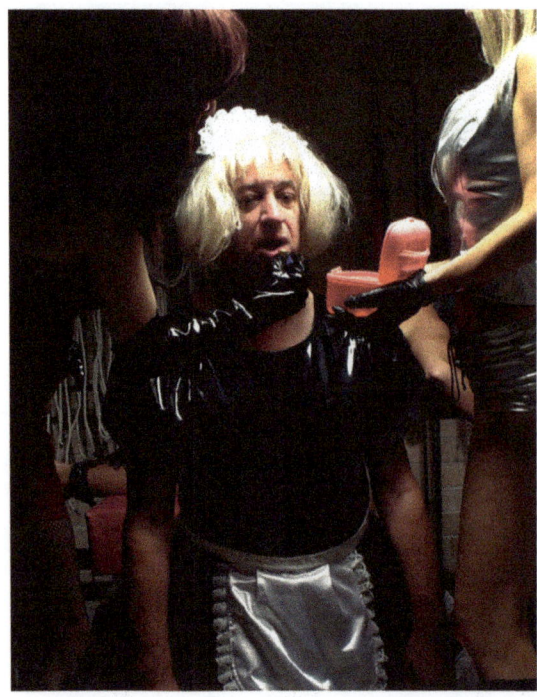

Once the makeup is to the satisfaction of the Domme/Dom, the dressing will be completed by a wig, preferably very long as most men may have difficulty in adjusting to suddenly having large amounts of hair about them.

Now that the dressing process is complete, the Domme/Dom can take the session through various other scenarios.

Specific Activity No. Seven: Enforced Public Humiliation

Public humiliation is an activity that has the potential to provide great stimulus to both the Domme/Dom and the sub. It does take courage, and careful planning.

While it is good to get a reaction from the public, the Domme/Dom must be careful not to get the wrong reaction. For example, it is acceptable to cross dress a male in street clothes and visit a shopping centre. It is not acceptable if he were to be dressed in a maid's uniform and the Domme/Dom led him by a chain attached to his cock and balls. This is likely to be considered offensive public behaviour and would not be long before the police were most likely called.

Public humiliation is most effective when the sub has absolutely no idea of the activity planned for the scenario, even to the extent that the role-play will be moving into the public arena at all.

Once the Domme/Dom announces they will be going out in public, perhaps the sub could be told they will be remaining in the relative obscurity of a car. That first step into public while in role will have a major impact on the sub, and that impact will be intensified if it is totally unexpected.

When moving role-play into the public arena, the Domme/Dom should keep a few points in mind when making decisions, such as:

- ✓ Where to go.
- ✓ What to do when they get there.
- ✓ What time to go to the selected venue.
- ✓ How long to stay.

SPECIFIC ACTIVITIES

Depending on the scenario being played, the Domme/Dom should select a venue that fits the appearance of both Domme/Dom and sub as well as the activities that are expected to be performed while at the venue. For example, there will be fewer restrictions on planned activities at a dance club on a Friday night than there will be at a suburban shopping centre on the Saturday morning before Christmas.

Also, to be considered is the possibility of accidentally meeting acquaintances (of either the Domme/Dom or the sub) at the chosen venue. This may be either a good meeting or a disastrous meeting, depending on the individuals involved.

If it is planned to visit an indoor venue (dance club, party, restaurant, etc.), the Domme/Dom needs to consider transport to and from the venue. Usually, transport will be via private vehicle, consideration should be given to parking availability at the venue, and the distance required to walk from the parked vehicle to the venue.

The Domme/Dom needs to plan exactly what the sub will be required to do once they arrive at the chosen venue. If the venue is a BDSM party, there will be an abundance of appropriate activities to occupy the sub's time, and there is little possibility of other party-goers being offended. However, if the venue is more public, such as a restaurant, shopping centre, or garden park, then fewer offensive activities must be organised. Simply because an activity is not publicly offensive does not mean that the sub will not suffer extreme embarrassment.

Obviously, depending on the venue selected, the Domme/Dom will arrange their excursion at the most appropriate time. Start times for particular events should be verified. Also, the Domme/Dom should verify if there is any variation of the normal operating hours for the particular venue (e.g. may be affected by public holidays).

Once at the chosen venue, the Domme/Dom must decide on the length of stay (this may be determined for them by unfavourable public reaction). At times, the conclusion will be dictated by the events themselves (e.g. the meal has been consumed, or the movie has ended). In other situations, the Domme/Dom must decide when the sub has had enough exposure (e.g. at the BDSM party, or simply walking down the street).

Public humiliation can take many forms of activities, types of venues, and times and lengths of visits. This is one area where the Domme/Dom can become creative with scenarios being forced onto the sub. When done properly, public humiliation of the sub is a most enjoyable activity.

Specific Activity No. Eight: Serving and Other Household Chores

Often in BDSM, serving and household chores will be enacted while the sub is dressed as a French maid (particularly effective for male subs). Alternatively, the sub may remain naked, or with minimal clothing such as latex jock strap or latex G-string. If, however, the sub was serving at the dinner table, and the Domme's/ Dom's guests were present, then it would be appropriate for the sub to be dressed as a French maid. The activity of domestic services, no matter who else may be in the house at the time, really emphasises dominance and superiority over the sub.

With newcomers to the BDSM scene, subs may be reluctant to experience heavier punishments such as canes, whips and clamps, and they opt for a softer approach to submission. This is quite acceptable, and the Domme/Dom can use this situation with a type of mental slavery and the threat of severe discipline. By opting for a light discipline role, the sub has established limits, it then becomes a challenge to the Domme/Dom to extend the limits for the sub, depending if the sub has agreed at the start to that activity.

Domestic services for the sub, while the Domme/Dom relaxes and is waited on may seem innocent enough, however this can become a powerful tool in establishing and maintaining the D/s relationship.

While performing domestic duties, the sub will wear the

SPECIFIC ACTIVITIES

clothing the Domme/Dom deems appropriate. The barest minimum should be slave collar, which should always be worn whenever the sub is in role. Clothing has already been discussed. It is quite acceptable for other items of restriction to be worn while performing domestic duties. These items may include hand cuffs, leg shackles, gag, plugs, and/or chastity devices.

Because some domestic duties may seem to be easy (e.g. dusting the furniture), the Domme/Dom may deliberately make things more interesting (or difficult) for the sub. While dusting the furniture may seem a simple exercise, it can become more interesting if the sub has their hands tied behind their back and the dusting is done with a cloth held in their mouth. It may become even more interesting if time limits are placed on the sub with failure or poor workmanship being rewarded with punishments.

In this type of scenario, the Domme/Dom has great flexibility in emphasising the respective roles in the D/s relationship.

# 29

Example Scenarios

The following pages contain examples of simple role-play scenarios. For the examples, our case study couple Mary and Fred will be used in situations where they will both be taking the submissive role. The examples are not complete scenarios from start to finish, but merely examples of what could be included in a larger overall role-play scene.

Role-play Example No. One: Starting a Role-play Session

By now, Mary and Fred they have been through a few test scenarios and have decided to purchase their start-up equipment. A spare bedroom in the house serves as their dungeon (or 'play room'), although role activities often take place in other areas in the house. Mary has settled into a more Dominant role, although from time to time she plans to switch so that she can try out new equipment from a sub's point of view (or should that be, point of discomfort?). Mary has opted for the simplistic role-play name of 'Mistress M, while she has named Fred 'subhuman'.

EXAMPLE SCENARIOS

Fred, meanwhile, is enjoying his submissive role, with the odd opportunity to play Dom over Mary. Fred has chosen his Dom name to be 'Sir Samson', while he has named the submissive Mary as 'nil'.

They already are very aware of each other's health and physical condition, each of them has filled out a checklist, and their respective limits have been established. No doubt the checklists and limits will be revisited as they become more experienced. They have agreed on the safe word of 'zebra'.

Mary has decided that she wants to place a full rope body harness on Fred as she really wants to become more proficient in the handling of ropes. She has discovered that while chains may be easier to use, the ropes really are more versatile. For this session she has notified Fred of her intentions by leaving a sealed envelope on the floor of the entry foyer inside the front door, so that when Fred returns home from work that evening, it would be the first thing he would see on entering the house. The envelope had only one word on the outside; 'subhuman'. When Fred arrived home and saw the envelope on the floor, his heart skipped a beat. He is always thrilled at the surprise of impromptu sessions. The envelope contained a single sheet of paper, containing the following instructions:

> "I expect you to be home and reading this by your usual time of 6:30pm. you will go directly to the play room, undress, and put on your slave collar. you will then assume a suitable slave position and await the pleasure of My arrival. Mistress M."

Fred glanced at his watch. It was 6:38 already! He ran towards the play room to follow the instructions of his Mistress.

Mary was reclining on her bed, reading a magazine, when she heard Fred arriving home. She listened as he opened the envelope and heard the flurry of activity as he rushed to the play room to carry out her instructions. She laughed quietly to herself and continued reading.

She waited almost half an hour before stirring. She rose from the bed and checked herself in the full-length wardrobe mirror. She was wearing a black leather bikini and over-the-knee black leather boots with 6" stiletto heels. She gathered up her riding crop and moved towards the play room.

Mary found Fred naked, except for the slave collar, and kneeling on the floor with his forehead touching the floor. His head was facing the direction of the door. She walked around him a few times, delivering a tirade of verbal abuse while she hit his exposed butt cheeks with her riding crop.

She ordered him to kneel upright while being mindful that he was not allowed to look at her face. She placed a latex gas mask over his head and re-adjusted the slave collar. He was instructed to stand upright.

From the rack containing all the ropes, Mary selected one of the longer ropes (six metres long).

EXAMPLE SCENARIOS

Role-play Example No. Two: Public Humiliation

Mary has decided to take Fred through a public humiliation scenario. She has not told him about her plan, and he is curious, he knows better than to question his Mistress. He trusts her.

She has him dressed in open-necked shirt and casual trousers, shoes and socks. Beneath this attire, he is invaded by a large butt plug that is held in place by tight latex shorts. His cock and balls are constricted. Nipple clamps are in place, and the customary slave collar is around his neck. From the D-ring at the front of the collar a chain leash is clipped, with the chain lead being concealed inside of the open neck shirt.

It is Saturday evening and Mary has driven them to a local restaurant area where all the restaurants offer sidewalk dining for their clients. The restaurants are at their capacity.

Mary parks the car and instructs Fred to get out. She passes him a mobile phone. She then delivers her instructions to a startled Fred:

"I will be staying on this side of the street, watching everything you do. You will cross over to the other side of the street. I will contact you by mobile phone if I need to give you further instructions. You will not attempt to conceal any of your bondage if it is showing. When on the other side of the street, you will ask people for the time. If they respond and give you the time, you will then fiddle with your neck collar, just to draw attention to it, thank them, and move on. You are required to convince five separate people to give you the time. You have just thirty minutes to complete this task.

Your time starts now, so don't stand there looking at me. Failure to complete this task will cause you severe discomfort when I get you home again."

Fred was terrified at this simple yet daunting task. The adrenalin was pumping as he crossed the street. He was terrified, yet excited by this challenge.

Role-play Example No. Three: Public Exhibitionism

Fred has decided to take Mary, as his sub, out for dinner. Fred had always considered Mary to be very attractive. He was always proud to take her out in public. Tonight, he wanted to put her exhibitionist tendencies to the test.

He had made a table reservation at the city's most exclusive restaurant. For socialites, this certainly was a place to be seen. Photographers were always milling around for that special snapshot for the gossip pages in Sunday's newspapers. This was a social gathering spot for the elite. Neither one of them had been here before. But tonight, was different!

Fred wore his dinner suit with black bow tie, mainly because men were not admitted unless they were dressed as such. His shoes were polished to mirror-like reflectiveness, and he wore a woollen overcoat to ward off the cool evening breeze.

Earlier in the week, Fred had purchased a dress for Mary, especially for this evening. The dress was black latex, highly polished, of course and deeply plunged at the front. The effect was maximum exposure of her cleavage as the strong latex material pushed her ample breasts upwards and inwards. Similarly, the dress only just managed to cover her butt cheeks. She tugged the dress downwards only to discover that she was risking freeing her breasts. The dress felt several sizes too small as it clung like glossy paint to her

EXAMPLE SCENARIOS

skin. She was wearing no underwear as the outlines would clearly show through the surface of the dress.

She also wore her thigh-high black patent leather boots with stiletto heels, as well long black latex gloves that almost reached up to her armpits. Around her neck was a simple leather collar.

Over this outfit she wore a tight-fitting corset and an ankle-length fur coat.

As they removed their coats and handed them to the valet at the front desk, the valet's eyes bulged at the site of Mary glistening in front of him. He handed them their valet ticket and they proceeded into the restaurant.

As the Maitre d' showed them to their table a stunned silence descended on the whole room. Women were shocked, and their men were drooling. The press cameras flashed.

In an instant, Mary had become the centre of attraction. She was proud of her physical attributes and her effect on others. She loved this attention.

Role-play Example No. Four: Bondage Parlour Visit

Mary liked the attention she received in public when Fred took her to dinner as his slave. Although she enjoyed the experience, it became apparent to them both, she really relished the role of

Mistress. Following the scenario debrief, both agreed she is a natural Domme. When Fred suggested the possibly of visiting a bondage parlour to gain some more experience alongside a professional Mistress, Mary happily agreed. Together, they researched a few places and decided on a reputable establishment as a good starting point. Mary wanted to learn more ways she could dish out punishments to Fred.

On the way to the parlour Mary's stomach was knotting with nervousness. Fred looked forward to the session with great anticipation and a certain amount of fear. He expected to experience pain intermingled with erotic pleasure that would carry him into his fantasy world.

Once they reached the front door and rang the bell, both knew it was the point of no return. The woman who opened the door took them by surprise, as she looked like she had stepped out of a corporate office. The only thing that associated her with the parlour was the collar around her neck, decorated with metal studs and small spikes. She led them to a large lounge area, a waiting room with a twist. Mary noticed a statue in the corner behind one of the leather armchairs, it was of a lady. She had one arm outstretched holding a set of iron shackles. These were something Mary had only seen in pictures. In another corner was a mannequin modelling a schoolgirl uniform. On the wall by the door was a placard explaining the 'house rules'. Hanging next to that was a poster detailing forthcoming scheduled BDSM parties. Another wall featured four framed photographs, all depicting parts of female anatomy that were all somehow shackled or bound.

Fred watched as Mary examined the contents of the room and asked her if she was ok, secretly hoping she did not want to run out the door.

Mary chose to stay, totally intrigued by the scene she was

witnessing before her eyes. It was one thing to see this scene in a magazine but now she was standing here, and it seemed so surreal. She felt fear and excitement at the same time. The lady who had opened the door earlier asked Mary to wait a few minutes while she gave Fred a checklist to fill out and directions to the bathroom where he was to shower, enter the dungeon and wait for the Mistress in a slave position until she arrived.

As Fred left the room, a few moments later, Mistress Karma strode into the room towards Mary, confident and commanding. She walked directly to her, embraced and kissed her on the cheek. She spoke with a soft warm voice, and Mary could not help thinking that this was not at all fitting with the image that this beautiful Mistress portrayed. Her confidence made Mary feel more at ease

Mary was suitably impressed. Mistress Karma was wearing a full-length black corset that had been tightly laced at the back. This was accompanied by black G-string underwear. The suspender straps from the corset were hitched to black fishnet stockings. She was wearing black patent leather knee-length boots with 6" (15cm) stiletto heels. The corset constricted her waist and gave the illusion of rounding out her buttocks and making her breasts appear to be larger than they really were. This achieved that fabled hourglass figure image.

Mistress Karma had flowing blond hair that was soft and well groomed. It contrasted nicely with the black outfit she was wearing. Her pale skin was unblemished. Her eyes were made up with an excessive use of eyeliner, mascara and grey eye shadow. Her lips were crimson, as were her nails. The colours around the eyes and on the lips again contrasted with the pale tones of her skin. She was heavily perfumed. It was an image that Mary considered would stir a reaction in most men. Mistress Karma came across as a professional and she commanded the room with authority and self-assurance. Mary somehow knew she could learn much from this experience with her.

As Mary followed her out, Mistress Karma asked Mary her Mistress name.

Mary answered, 'Mistress M'.

Mistress Karma announced that Mary would be called that name from now till the end of the session. She pointed to a closed door at the end of the hall, letting Mary know this was the dungeon where they would be carrying out their little scenario with Fred.

Mary was ushered into a room where she had trouble concentrating on the instructions she had been given. She was busily trying to absorb and understand the sight before her. There was a double bed in the room. There were no pillows on the bed, shackles attached to each corner of the bed. Against one wall stood a large wooden cross in the shape of an 'X'. Shackles were attached to each of the extremities of the cross with ring bolts down both sides. Another wall contained racks featuring an assortment of paddles, straps, ropes, gags, blindfolds and collars.

Mary was ready to be transformed into Mistress M. She unhooked her bra, allowing her breasts to bounce free. She was now wearing nothing, but a red latex G-string Fred had purchased for her. Mistress Karma walked across to the small table by the bed and picked up a red latex skirt to match. She powdered the inside of it to make it easier to glide up Mary's legs and over her hips. The skirt moulded itself onto her body. It felt tight and constricting, yet it stretched so easily with her movement. It barely reached the cheeks of her butt, let alone cover them. She admired herself in the full-length mirror and could not believe how this texture felt

EXAMPLE SCENARIOS

and moved with her. It was as though it had been painted on. She felt sexy. Mistress Karma was taking in the vision before her as a smile hovered over her lips.

Next was the latex top Mistress Karma was holding open for her, as one does for a coat to be donned. Mary turned her back to Karma and then slipped her arms through the small sleeve openings, turning back around to face Mistress Karma allowing her to move the front zipper all the way up to the plunging neckline of the top. The tight constricting latex fabric clearly outlined her ample breasts and her nipples, which were showing through. Mary looked back at the mirror and a sexy vision bounced back at her. She was now transformed into Mistress M.

Mistress Karma began wiping smudges of the powder from the latex using a small hand towel.

'Slave will finish the rest,' she said. Mary examined herself in the mirror one more time, then followed Mistress Karma from the room and towards the main dungeon.

When the door to the dungeon was opened, in an instant Mary was overwhelmed by the atmosphere of this room. She quickly cast her gaze around the dungeon, trying to absorb as much as she could. Her hurried initial inspection of the equipment revealed several wall-mounted railings and hooks. Hanging from these were a vast assortment of collars, blindfolds, gags, cuffs and straps. In the corner stood a metal stand containing dildos, butt plugs, lubricant, condoms, bottles of disinfectant, tissues and small hand towels. Along the back wall of the room a hammock was suspended from the ceiling.

Closer inspection revealed that this was an unusual hammock as the base could only support the torso of the occupant. The base itself looked to be made from very sturdy leather. It was suspended by large link chains from the ceiling and each of the chains had a cuff attached, presumably, Mary thought, for the wrists and ankles of the occupant. Next along the wall was a large set of wooden stocks with holes for the neck and wrists, plus cuffs to support legs and ankles.

In the far corner was a chain that led up to a pulley hanging from the ceiling. The chain dangling down from the pulley suspended an iron bar that had wrist cuffs attached to each of its ends. The chain and pulley obviously were for lowering and raising the iron bar. Behind the chain leading up to the pulley were more wall-mounted railings, this time containing a myriad of ropes in an assortment of colours and lengths. Beside the ropes were a series of mannequin heads that all displayed full head masks, some made of leather and other of latex. Next was a large high-backed wooden chair, resembling a throne. Beside this in the corner were more heads with masks and a large terracotta vase containing more than a dozen canes and two large feathers. To the left, the wall was adorned by various long-tailed and short-tailed whips. Full length floor to ceiling mirrors were used at different points on each of the four walls and the floor was tiled with dark grey slate. The dungeon was lit by at least a dozen large candles placed at strategic points around the room.

The impact on Mary was both sudden and dramatic. It was as though she had stepped into another world. Mistress Karma had turned and was watching her reaction. She was smiling broadly and enjoying the moment of introducing a novice to her world of Domination. Mary closed the door behind her and stepped further into the room. She looked down and saw Fred on his knees in the centre of the dungeon, leaning forward, his nose and forehead touching the floor with his arms outstretched before him, palms facing upwards. He was totally naked.

EXAMPLE SCENARIOS

Mistress Karma selected a leather slave collar from the rack on the wall and while fastening it around his neck, she slipped into the role of ridiculing her slave boy with a voice that had now taken a more threatening and commanding tone.

Mistress Karma was carrying a riding crop in her right hand as she slowly trailed the leather end of the crop over Fred's back and around his exposed buttocks. In an instant, the crop flicked. It smacked against Fred's flesh and an imprint of the crop was left emblazoned on Fred's left buttock. Mistress Karma laughed aloud as the crop flicked again and a matching imprint appeared on his right buttock. Mary flinched at the smacking sounds of both impacts.

Fred did not move, nor did he emit any sounds. Mistress Karma motioned for Mary to move forward until she was standing directly in front of Fred, with toes of her shoes almost touching his outstretched fingertips. Once Mary was in position, Karma continued with her commands to Fred.

She instructed him to clean Mary's (now Mistress M's) shoes with his tongue, showing his adoration by kissing her legs only up as high as her knees. He was not permitted to look either Mistress in the face, nor permitted to speak without asking permission first. Fred raised his head slightly and nodded to indicate his understanding of Her instructions while Mistress Karma gave him two more smacks with the riding crop because he was taking too long.

Mary could not believe what was happening before her eyes, or at least, at her feet. Mistress Karma passed the riding crop to Mary as slave began washing her left shoe with his tongue. Mistress Karma continued to give instructions to Mary, motioning her to hit slave with the crop. As she took a swing it connected with his right buttock, but not squarely. Mary took a second swing, this time with a more pleasing smack on the other buttock, while uttering her first command for the slave to go faster, because she did not have all day.

This was followed by two more swings of the crop, both of which left flaming pink imprints on the upturned buttocks in front of her. She gazed with amusement at the pattern of crop marks being displayed on Fred's butt. Mistress Karma gave Fred a bottle and a cloth while barking orders for him to polish Mistress M's latex. slave quickly crawled back to Mistress M with the bottle of lubricant in one hand and the polishing cloth in the other. Immediately he squirted some of the lubricant onto her skirt and top and began wiping the surface clean using the cloth with vigorous yet gentle strokes.

Mistress M looked to one of the mirrors and was amazed at her image. Her latex was glistening and dancing in the flickering candlelight. It looked very much like she was wearing nothing but wet body paint as the outfit stretched and hugged her contours, moving easily when she moved. From that instant, Mistress M became a devoted fan of latex. slave crawled back towards Mistress Karma and he replaced the bottle of lubricant and cleaning cloth to their positions on the metal stand in the corner. he crawled back to be at Mistress Karma's feet to await his next command.

Mistress Karma reached down and snap-clipped a leash onto the D-ring at the front of the slave's collar. She handed the end of the leash to Mistress M. Mistress Karma pointed to a spot directly under the metal bar swinging from the chain on the pulley and asked Mistress M to take slave there. She strode over to the designated spot, tugging slave along behind her. Mistress Karma moved to where the chain was anchored on the wall hook. She released the chain and it ran through the pulley with a loud clanking noise.

The metal bar lowered to approximately Mistress

EXAMPLE SCENARIOS

M's head height, leaving the bar swaying at a convenient working height. slave was commanded to stand with his eyes fixed on the floor at his feet. Mistress Karma removed the dog leash from his slave collar and hung it back on a wall rack. She returned to slave, holding two cotton balls that she squeezed into his ears. She then covered his head with a latex mask. The slave collar had to be removed and re-attached so that it was on top of the neck part of the latex hood. The hood itself was open-faced and did not cover the eyes, nose or mouth.

Mistress Karma attended to these shortcomings by quickly slipping an elasticized blindfold over his head and by pushing a leather ball gag into his mouth. Due to slave's inability to utter a word because of the gag, Mistress M already knew his safe exit if he got into strife physically and needed an out. he was to shake his head as hard as he could to alert Mistress of his need for immediate halt to the session.

Next, his hands were buckled into the wrist straps at either of the metal bar that was swaying in front of his bound head. Mistress Karma went to one of the wall racks and returned with a longer metal bar with straps attached at each end, and she stood behind slave. With her hand, she smacked him several times on the insides of his thighs, and immediately he spread his feet wide apart. She knelt down and positioned the bar between his feet and secured his ankles into the straps at each end of the bar.

Satisfied with her efforts, Mistress Karma walked back to where the chain was anchored on the wall and began to pull the chain back towards her. The pulley clanked again, and the chain began to raise the bar slowly. slave's arms were raised with the bar. Mistress M watched with amusement. Soon, slave's arms were outstretched above his head.

Awkwardly, he shuffled his feet so that he was directly under the bar. Mistress M watched his heels begin to lift, leaving him balancing on his toes.

Mistress Karma anchored the chain to the wall hook. Mistress M was amused to see that slave's penis was erect, begging for attention from these two beautiful Mistresses. He could not hear any conversations now that he had his ears plugged and wearing a latex mask, nor could he see anything that was about to take place. Mistress M stood there in disbelief, unable to comprehend what she was seeing. Her eyes twinkled at the notion of learning some basic discipline activities.

With the careful instruction and supervision by Mistress Karma, Mistress M began by smacking her slave's left buttock cheek with her hand. It was an unusual slapping motion of upwards and downwards. The slaps were coming in rapid succession as her hand flashed over the exposed buttock. She was careful not to miss the target.

The process was soon repeated on the other buttock. Mistress M noticed both of slave's cheeks had turned a light pink and the imprints of the crop were still clearly visible. A smile crept up on her face; she was pleased with her handywork. Mistress Karma handed Mistress M what looked like a small whip. It had a short-polished handle and maybe twenty or thirty tails made of very soft brushed leather coming out from the handle. This was called a flogger and could be used all over the body without too much damage.

Mistress M tried it on her own leg and was surprised to find that it left a mild tingling sensation. She began using it, first on his buttocks, then on his back and on the backs of slave's legs. She moved around and flogged him across his chest, stomach and the front of his legs. Even though she was putting considerable force into some of the strokes,

EXAMPLE SCENARIOS

there was no noticeable reaction from slave. Mistress Karma was ready to step it up a notch, with a short leather strap attached to a short handle she positioned herself behind slave and swung the strap in a backhand motion. There was a resounding slap as leather met flesh and this time, slave flinched. He did not expect the blow, squirming, unable to escape, nor able to hear or see it was coming. Mistress Karma handed Mistress M a strap and control while she went to retrieve the next toy to be used on their helpless slave.

Mistress M swung the strap, alternating between the cheeks and taking her time, ensuring that she struck the intended target area. slave was now flinching with each hit and his cheeks had changed from a light pink to a dull red. Mistress Karma returned with a container of talcum powder and while sprinkling and smoothing it over slave's red buttocks, She explained the soothing and coolness on his cheeks would better prepare him for the punishment yet to come.

The next toy was a round paddle, looking very similar to a ping-pong bat, obviously much sturdier. Mistress Karma began spanking his buttocks one at a time. Residual powder swirled as the paddle struck slave with dull thuds, causing him to rock on his toes and sway in his bonds. He was now showing signs of some discomfort. Mistress Karma handed Mistress M a riding crop and watched as Mistress M was striking blows to the now bright red cheeks. This was known as a warm-up process, getting the blood circulating in the slave. Mistress Karma explained that if you go to the heavier punishment without the warm-up the slave will not be able to endure the punishment for as long. It would be over too quickly.

By now slave jerked forward at each impact and uttered a small grunt of agony. While laughing, Mistress M found this curiously satisfying. slave's reactions pleased her. Mistress Karma had returned carrying a single cane. Mistress M stepped back to give her room to work and better observe her in action. Mistress Karma gently ran her hand over slave's flaming butt, by now sensitive to even the slightest touch, and he flinched when her hand caressed his tortured skin.

She then stepped to one side and held the cane at the spot where she intended to strike. The cane was not quite touching his skin, so he would not be aware of where or when the strike would be delivered. He didn't have long to wait. The cane flicked back, forward, then back again. slave jerked forward, momentarily losing his footing while emitting a muffled scream from behind his gag. Mistress was now taking her time, giving slave a chance to recompose himself while she was taking careful aim for the next strike. This method also gave him an agonising wait for the next inevitable blow while she stepped away, leaving him wondering for a minute.

Satisfied with her performance and his glowing cheeks, she decided it was time for a new position. Meanwhile, Mistress M was bewildered at the level of intensity and was not prepared for this. She knew slave was able to be released from this bondage at his own mercy and was surprised at the amount of punishment he was able to withstand.

Mistress Karma unhooked the chain and began lowering the suspension bar, unshackled his wrists and removed the spreader bar from his ankles. slave began flexing both arms and legs in relief. The collar, latex hood, blindfold and gag were all left in place. She guided him over to the long vinyl-topped table with strategically placed holes in it that was against the wall, pushed his upper body over it and grabbed one of his ankles and lifted it, he got the message to lie face down.

EXAMPLE SCENARIOS

    She walked to the other end of the table and grabbed both wrists and extended them fully above his head and attached them to the cuffs. Moving to his side, she pushed him on his hip where he wriggled towards the centre. She knelt down to look underneath, satisfied she stood up. Mistress M had been observing this process with keen interest and she marvelled at the ease which Mistress Karma commanded her subject.

    Mistress Karma proceeded to wrap leather restraints around his ankles. The restraints were attached by chains to the roller at the foot of the table. She gave the roller about half a turn then locked it into place. She moved to the head of the table, similarly restrained his wrists and began turning the roller slowly. Mary realised that slave was now secured and fully extended on a torture rack. Mistress Karma turned the roller until he was stretched to the point where any movement appeared extremely unlikely and then the roller was locked in place. She then wound wide leather straps over his body and under the table. These straps were simply secured by roller buckles. One strap covered the upper part of his back and the other covered the small of his back. Smaller straps were wound around his thighs but were threaded through slots in the table rather than covering the whole width of the table. These had the effect of immobilising his upper legs and at the same time keeping the thighs spread wide apart. Mistress Karma retrieved more implements from the wall racks. The first was a piece of string. She knelt down under the table and motioned for Mistress M to join her.

    Under the table Mistress M discovered that slave's genitals were fully exposed, courtesy of a convenient slot cut into the table top. Mistress Karma grabbed slave's scrotum and began tying the string around it and in doing so, separated his testicles. The ends of the string were tied to a bar between the legs of the foot of the table. The string was pulled taut when the final knot was tied. Mistress Karma moved towards the head of the table, reached into two more slots, found slave's nipples, pulled them into position. She attached clamps to each of his nipples.

slave screamed through his gag. The nipple clamps were attached to each other by a chain and to this chain she clipped a weight bag and let it drop. slave screamed again, this time louder and longer. Mistress Karma stood up to observe her handiwork. She explained that to give out effective canning it is best to have a slave totally immobilised, so he cannot twist and squirm while one is trying to hit the target area.

Two bath towels were placed on slave's back, one above his buttocks and another placed on his thighs immediately under his buttocks. This ensures the target area is well defined. With heavy punishment it is crucial not to damage the kidneys, particularly if you hit too high. Mistress M was excited by the prospect of her slave sporting her bruises in the days to come. She selected a thinner cane as she knew this would sting more than the thicker ones.

Mistress Karma took her arm and showed her the right height to hold the cane, guiding her arm slowly downward so that the cane rested lightly on the target, then lifting her arm to the original height again. She instructed Mistress M to practice this motion a few times, pointing out that hitting hard doesn't necessarily get the desired impact. You are still able to get good results by a flick of the wrist at the point of impact.

As Mistress M tried a few more practice swings, the cane was making swishing sounds as she flicked it around. Mistress M was pleasantly surprised she enjoyed listening to

EXAMPLE SCENARIOS

this sound and made a mental note to purchase one of these on their next shopping trip. Standing in position by her slave, Mistress M raised her cane as instructed and swung. The blow landed almost entirely on the towel placed on slaves' lower back. She swung again, this time it was another ill-directed blow to the side of his right buttock. This is not as easy as she thought. She was relishing the thought of needing a lot of practice to get it right.

By the time Mistress M had swung the cane ten times, she found that she was able to strike the target, pretty close to the exact spot where she intended to hit. She was developing a pattern of angry red welts on his cheeks. Each hit was rewarded with a muffled scream from slave, as he was totally unable to move to avoid her attack. Mistress M gladly obliged Mistress Karma with six more strokes, as directed, feeling more confident with each stroke. Mistress M was feeling proud of herself, she was really enjoying this scenario.

Mistress Karma bent under the table and removed the nipple clamps. This brought more screams from slave as the blood rushed back into his crushed nipples. She then freed his scrotum from the restraining string. She stood over the table and released the locked rollers before unshackling his wrists and ankles and the straps around his torso and thighs.

Mistress Karma rolled him over on his back and re-applied the restraints to his wrists and ankles. She adjusted the rollers to stretch him out again and again locked the rollers in place. He was still wearing the latex hood, the slave collar, the blindfold and the gag.

Mistress Karma thanked Mistress M for participating in the introduction to the world of Domination and wished her the very best in her future sessions with slave. She was now handing slave over to Mistress M to finish him off, however she pleased. She instructed them to have showers, dress and buzz the intercom when they were done. After bidding them farewell, Mistress Karma left the dungeon, closing the door behind her.

Mistress M examined her slave still lying helplessly on the table, now facing upwards and unable to move, bound and gagged. His penis was erect, waiting for her. Without undressing, Mistress M climbed up onto the table, straddling her slave. Her skirt was so short that she merely had to fold the hemline up a few centimetres to achieve what she wanted now. She was feeling moist and wanted sex badly. Here was an opportunity to get what she wanted, no more, no less, and exactly on her terms, with no objection whatsoever from her partner. She had never imagined that this was at all possible.

She glided her body up and over his outstretched torso. She grabbed his shaft and guided its head into her wet sex. She left it there for a couple of seconds then pulled it out. he groaned loudly with frustration. She sat back on his thighs and laughed, soaking up every enjoyable second of this game. After a minute, she guided the tip of his shaft into her again, and again withdrew after a couple of seconds, another groan and another laugh. She looked across the room to a large wall mirror. She gazed at the image of a bitch Mistress barely clad in glossy latex tormenting and controlling her helpless slave boy.

For a moment she was transfixed, unable to tear her eyes away. Was that really the shy and demure Mary? The bitch in the mirror stared back at her. It was an image that was burned into her memory, never to be forgotten.

Finally, she could hold back no longer, and moved her body up over her slave and impaled herself on his shaft. She moved rhythmically on him, slowly at first but then increasing the tempo. Normally he would now be pumping with her, but he was unable to move to increase his sexual enjoyment. She had him bound and in her control. She was working harder, bouncing up and down on him, emitting small screams of pleasure. He was groaning non-stop with similar pleasure but also with the frustration of being bound during this moment of intimate ecstasy. They climaxed simultaneously.

Role-play Example No. Five: Activities for a dinner party scenario

Since Mary's visit to the parlour, she has not stopped thinking about the events and how much she enjoyed the feeling of being in total control of another person in this way. After the session, Mistress Karma, whom she trained with, mentioned that perhaps Mary might like to attend a private dinner party at her home, so Mary could gain some more experiences as a Mistress. At the time, Mary's response was that she needed to go away and process what she had witnessed but found herself thinking about the parties more and more. Fred was delighted and very excited at this prospect and left it up to Mary to organise when she was ready.

It did not take Mary long to decide she would like to experience a dinner party as a Mistress with slaves. When speaking to Mistress Karma on the phone, Mary suggested Fred be the slave. Mistress Karma agreed and said she would also have her slave and two sissy maids (who would be serving food and making sure the dinner party ran smoothly) present. Following is the scenario of the dinner party.

Activities for the Dinner Party
Attendees:

Mistresses:
Mistress M
Mistress Karma

sissy maids:
celeste
celine

slave boys:
Fred (as subhuman)
zed (Mistress Karma's slave)

The schedule for the evening's events are as follows:

4pm: Mary arrives with Fred. His name for the night is 'subhuman'. he is branded, blindfolded and bound, then placed in cage to wait with slave zed, who is already bound, blindfolded and gagged, sitting in the cage. This allows both Mistresses time to discuss in another room the limits of both slaves, including the safe words.

5pm: mummification of slave zed to begin, while blindfold of slave subhuman is removed, so he can watch from inside the cage and constantly being threatened that he is next for mummification. ***Mistresses keep an eye out for the mummified slave the whole time he is bound. During this time ensuring his breathing is normal, he is given sips of water, making sure he is not distressed and is safe (before participating in this scenario, read the disclaimer at the beginning of this manual). This is a dangerous scenario, precautions are needed, and you need to take responsibility for your actions. This is another reason drugs and alcohol should not be taken before or during session). Also see the effective mummification process in chapter twenty eight of specific activities**

6pm: sissy maids arrive, they dress up in their complete maid uniforms and after careful inspection by the Mistresses, they begin preparing drinks and snacks before dinner.

EXAMPLE SCENARIOS

Meanwhile slave subhuman is let out of cage, unbound and attending to the personal needs of the Mistresses such as massaging their feet and any other desires of the Mistresses.

7pm: Dinner is served by sissy maids while subhuman sits under the table on all fours and waits while Mistresses eat and place their feet on his back using him as a foot stool. They may direct him to massage feet. During the meal the Mistresses hurl insults towards the slave to make him feel subhuman. For Mistress' entertainment, subhuman may be asked to place an extra weight around sub zeds genitals who is mummified and standing.

8pm: sissy maids clean up dinner table and wash up, as well as provide tea/coffee and refreshments as directed by Mistresses while slave subhuman is ridiculed and disciplined

8.45pm: Mistresses begin releasing zed from mummification with the help of sissy maids and slave subhuman, then maids clean him up.

9.30pm: sissy maids, subhuman and zed are directed to eat while sitting on kitchen floor. sissy maids only use their fingers, no utensils allowed, while subhuman and slave zed have their hands lightly bound behind their back and served scraps in a dog bowl (the timer is set to 15min to eat and wash up). There is punishment for all four if they don't finish within 15 minutes.

9.45pm: sissy maids and subhuman are inspected after washing up, making sure they have completed tasks on time. sissy maids will be lined up for critical assessment by the Mistresses. Generally, discipline follows this as they certainly would not have had enough time to complete tasks and even so, Mistresses don't need a reason to inflict discipline on their subs.

10pm: Let the games begin!
    slave push-ups for one minute, then spanking for not doing them correctly and repeating process.
    10.10pm: ring the dildo
    10.40pm: slave sprints
    10.50pm: serving fruit for the Mistresses
    11.15pm: slave rides
    11.45pm: worth the weight

EXAMPLE SCENARIOS

Midnight: discipline session for sissy maids and slave boys, all slaves and maids into the cage and allowed out one at a time for discipline in the playroom.

1am: slaves and sissy maids tidy and clean the area and allowed to come out of role and shower only when Mistresses are satisfied they have sufficiently cleaned up to the Mistresses standards.

Description of games

Ring the Dildo

- slaves are placed in the laundry while furniture is re-arranged to become obstacles in the game.
- slave boy is blindfolded with his hands cuffed behind his back. He is led out to the middle of the room and is turned around to disorient him.
- he must move unassisted to the play room.
- Each time he bumps into furniture or walls, he must take one large pace backwards and bend over to receive one stroke of the cane from his dissatisfied Mistress and not forgetting to thank her before continuing.
- The slaves' Mistress may stand behind him to give him directions left or right.
- Once in the playroom, the slave must kneel and pick up a cock ring from the floor with his teeth.
- The slave must bring the cock ring back to the middle of the room from where he started, if he drops it he must repeat the whole exercise from the start.
- Upon returning to the starting area, he must slide the cock ring over the dildo on the floor, as directed by the Mistress.
- Both slaves will be timed, and they get 15min each to complete the task, the slave with the longest time to the finish gets a spanking by his Mistress.

slave sprints

- Each slave will take turns on the treadmill until he begs for mercy.
- slaves will have their hands in arm binders and secured behind them and they will be wearing a gas mask.
- The same setting will be set for each slave.
- slave who stays on longest, wins.
- The slave to finish last gets a spanking by his Mistress or whatever the Mistress desires.

Fruit for the Mistresses

- Each slave will take a turn and be timed wearing long arm binders tied behind his back.
- slave will have to bring two lemons from the floor at one end of the room to his Mistress seated at the other end of the room.
- Punishment for the slave who does not complete this task within specified timeframe.

slave rides

- Each slave will take turns at transporting his own Mistress around a designated course, this will be done by the slave on his hands and knees.
- slave will be blindfolded and have an attachment of weights to his genitals.
- The Mistress will ride on the slaves back directing by using reigns or the riding crop.

EXAMPLE SCENARIOS

Worth the weight

- slave is blindfolded with hands cuffed behind his back.
- Nipple clamps are applied with a 25g weight sack attached.
- The weight sack is placed between the slave's teeth.
- Mistresses will try to get the slave boy to drop the weight sack out of his mouth.
- Mistresses cannot touch the face of the slave boy nor his genitals.
- Mistresses cannot touch the nipple clamps nor the weight sack in slaves' mouth.
- Once the weight is dropped, the slaves time is recorded and the slave with the shortest amount of time gets punished.

Glossary of Terms

Twenty-four/seven	24 hours a day, seven days a week (full-time!) where the sub lives with and is controlled by the Domme/Dom on a full-time basis
BDSM	Bondage Discipline Sadism Masochism
Body worship	to kiss and/or lick the Domme's/Dom's body
Bondage	the practise of tying or restraining
Boot worship	to kiss or lick the boots or shoes being worn by the Domme/Dom
bottom	same as sub
Butt plug	an object with a flared edge that is inserted in the anus
CBT	cock and ball torture
Chastity belt	a belt designed to be locked to prevent a person from having sexual intercourse or performing masturbation

GLOSSARY OF TERMS

Clamps	clips, often metal, which are attached to the nipples or genitals
Collar	worn around the neck to symbolise submissiveness or slavery to a Domme/Dom
Consensual	based on mutual agreement, not coerced
Crop	standard horsewhip – causes significant pain and leaves marks, even when lightly applied
Cuffs	either metal or leather and worn on the wrists and/or ankles as a method of restraint
Discipline	practice which causes discomfort for sexual or emotional arousal
Dom	a Dominant role for a Male (also known as Master)
Domme	a Dominant role for a Female (also known as Domina or Dominatrix)
Domination	includes obeying instructions, carrying out tasks, humiliation, and being dominated generally by a Domme/Dom – principally it is psychological play
Dungeon	BDSM play room
D/s	Dominant/submissive relationship

Enema	used to fill the colon with water – often used as a prerequisite to anal play, and/or in medical scenes
Fantasy	a BDSM scene that is desired by the role-players to be enacted
Fetish	used to describe a specific area of interest in BDSM
Flogger	rubber, latex or leather multi-stranded whip
Gag	any device used to prevent the submissive from speaking
Golden shower	the act of being urinated upon
Harness	leather or rope around the torso, constricting the body and restricting movements
Hood	masks that totally enclose the head
Humiliation	physical or mental degradation of the submissive
Latex	soft, thin rubber that can be polished to a high glossy finish
Limits	boundaries of consent as negotiated between partners, including activities in which one person does not wish to participate

GLOSSARY OF TERMS

Maid training	wearing a French maid's uniform – cleaning, serving the Domme/Dom, and generally acting as a maid
Masochist	a person who enjoys receiving intense sensation in a consensual and erotic BDSM scene
Master	same as Dom
Medical scenes	where the Domme/Dom plays the role of doctor or nurse and where the submissive is the patient
Mistress	same as Domme
Mummification	the entire body is tightly wrapped in cling plastic or other suitable wrapping material or enclosed in a body bag – breathing is regulated by means of a mouth or nose tube
Nipple torture	any application of pain to the nipples
Play	to participate in a BDSM scene
PVC	a synthetic plastic material used for some items of BDSM clothing
Restraints	cuffs, leather or metal, that enclose around the wrists, ankles, thighs, and/or waist

Role-play	where both Domme/Dom and sub are acting out parts in the BDSM scene – almost all BDSM involves some level of role-play
Rubber	same as latex
SSC	abbreviation for safe, sane, and consensual
Sadist	a person who enjoys giving intense pain in a consensual BDSM scene
Safe word	the word to be used to bring role-play to an instant stop (usually because of some difficulty for the sub, or the passing of pre-defined boundaries)
Scene	refers to actively engaging in BDSM role play
Sensory deprivation	the use of toys to remove input from the sub's senses
slave	a person who is consensually owned as property of a Domme/Dom
Spreader bars	a rigid bar attached to ankle cuffs or wrist cuffs, designed to hold the legs or arms apart (a broom handle cut to the desired length and with eye bolts on each end may be used also)
St Andrew's cross	a diagonal cross upon which the submissive is tied

GLOSSARY OF TERMS

sub	or submissive – plays the role opposite the Domme/Dom in the BDSM scene
subspace	a trance-like euphoric state in the submissive partner
Suspension	being hung up, or suspended, by tied wrists, ankles, and/or waist
Switch	a role-player who will take either a dominant or a sub role
Top	same as Domme or Dom
Vanilla sex	standard (missionary position) sex without BDSM

Appendix A

Sample Checklist

The following pages contain a template of a submissive checklist. Such checklists are useful for any type of D/s relationship. From novice to an experienced player.

The Domme/Dom should present this list for the sub to complete. Providing that the sub is completely honest when supplying the answers, the Domme/Dom will be able to build an accurate picture of the sub's experiences and expectations and likes and dislikes.

The checklist nominates a wide range of activities. The sub needs to provide three answers to each. For each activity, the sub must answer one of the following:

- ✓ **Experienced?** ….. (Yes no, or not applicable to gender)
- ✓ **Willingness to participate?** ….. (as often as possible, like on a regular basis, like on occasional basis, no special appeal, don't like but will do, will do only if Domme/Dom really wants it, outside of personal limits, or don't understand)
- ✓ **Comment** …. a brief comment from the sub on each activity

APPENDIX A

Comments from the sub are important for the Domme/Dom. For example, for cross dressing, the comment might be 'would be humiliating', or for whipping the comment might be 'do not draw blood' or 'do not break the skin'. This is all information for the Domme/Dom to use in session while respecting the requirements of the sub.

The Domme/Dom may also use the comments column to indicate activities that are outside the limits of the Domme/Dom, and in fact, there are examples of this displayed on the sample checklist. Even though the Domme/Dom may have nominated a particular activity as being outside limits, the sub should still answer the questions. If this happens to be an activity that the sub really wants, then maybe the Domme/Dom will alter the boundaries to have the activity included in the role-play.

Be aware that the activities listed on the checklist template are an attempt to cover most known activities in the BDSM scene. Dommes/Doms will have to decide for themselves where their own personal boundaries lie.

The aspects of safety, health and hygiene must always remain paramount when deciding whether to include various activities in role-play scenarios. The Domme/Dom must address these aspects when defining limits and must always be aware of the dangers when in actual role-play scenarios.

BOUND FOR PLAY - BDSM TRAINING MANUAL

(slave name here) (date here)

THE KEY:

Have you ever done this activity? (Yes or No) – X if it does not apply to your gender

Willingness:
- 5 = A wild turn-on – often as possible please
- 4 = I like doing this on a regular basis
- 3 = I usually like this on an occasional basis
- 2 = I am willing to do this but has no special appeal
- 1 = I don't like this, but won't object if asked to do it
- 0 = I don't like this and will object – I will only do it if Domme/Dom really wants it
- NO = I will not do this under any circumstances
- ? = I don't understand what this is

Experience: Willingness to participate:

Activity	Y	N	X	5	4	3	2	1	0	N	?	Comments
abrasion												
age play												
anal sex												
anal plugs (small)												
anal plugs (large)												
anal plugs (public, under clothes)												
animal roles												

APPENDIX A

arm and leg sleeves (binders)										
asphyxiation										
auctioned for charity										
ball stretching										
bathroom use control										
beating (soft)										
beating (hard)										
blindfolds										
being serviced (sexually)										
being bitten										
breast/chest bondage										
breath control										
branding										
boot worship										
bondage (light)										
bondage (heavy)										
bondage (multi-day)										
bondage (public, under clothing)										
breast whipping										
brown showers										
cages (locked inside of)										
caning										

castration fantasy									
catheterisation									
cattle prod (electrical toy)									
closets (locked inside of)									
chains									
chamber pot use									
chastity belts									
chauffeuring									
choking									
chores (domestic service)									
clothespins									
cock rings/ straps									
cock worship									
collars (worn in private)									
collars (worn in public)									
competitions (with other subs)									
corsets (wearing casually)									
corsets (trained waist reduction)									
cross dressing									

APPENDIX A

cuffs (leather)										
cuffs (metal)										
cutting										
diapers (wearing)										
diapers (wetting)										
diapers (soiling)										
dilation										
dildos										
double penetration										
electricity										
enemas (for cleansing)										
enemas (retention/ punishment)										
enforced chastity										
erotic dance (for audience)										
examinations (physical)										
exercise (forced/ required)										
exhibitionism (friends)										
exhibitionism (strangers)										
eye contact restrictions										
face slapping										

fantasy abandonment									
fantasy rape									
fantasy gang rape									
fear									
fisting (anal)									
fisting (vaginal)									
flame play									
flogging (giving)									
flogging (receiving)									
following orders									
foot worship									
forced bedwetting									
forced dressing									
forced eating									
forced homosexuality									
forced masturbation									
forced nudity (private)									
forced nudity (around others)									
forced servitude									
full head hoods									
gags (cloth)									
gags (inflatable)									

APPENDIX A

gags (phallic)									
gags (rubber)									
gags (tape)									
gas masks									
gates of hell (male genital torture)									
genital sex									
given to another Dom (temp)									
given to another Dom (perm)									
golden showers									
hair pulling									
hand jobs (giving)									
hand jobs (receiving)									
harems (serving with other subs)									
harnessing (leather)									
harnessing (rope)									
having food chosen for you									
having clothing chosen for you									
head (give fellatio/ cunnilingus)									

BOUND FOR PLAY - BDSM TRAINING MANUAL

head (receive fellatio/ cunnilingus)								
high heel wearing								
high heel worship								
homage with tongue								
hoods								
hot oils (on genitals)								
hot waxing								
housework (doing)								
human puppy dog								
humiliation (private)								
humiliation (public)								
hypnotism								
ice cubes								
immobilisation								
infantilism								
initiation rites								
injections								
intricate (Japanese) rope bondage								
interrogations								
kidnapping fantasy								

APPENDIX A

kneeling									
knife play									
leather clothing									
leather restraints									
lectures for misbehaviour									
licking (non-sexual)									
lingerie (wearing)									
manacles and irons									
manicures (giving)									
massage (giving)									
massage (receiving)									
medical scenes									
modelling for erotic photos									
mummification									
name change (for scene)									
name change (legal, permanent)									
nipple clamps									
nipple rings (piercing)									
nipple play/torture									
nipple weights									

oral/anal play								
over-the-knee spanking								
orgasm denial								
orgasm control								
outdoor scenes								
outdoor sex								
pain (mild)								
pain (medium)								
pain (severe)								
persona training (in scene)								
phone sex (serving Domme/Dom)								
phone sex (serving friends)								
phone sex (commercial providers)								
piercing (temp, play pierce)								
piercing (permanent)								
prison scenes								
prostitution (public pretence)								
prostitution (actual)								
pony slave								
public exposure								

APPENDIX A

punishment scene									
pussy/cock whipping									
pussy worship									
riding crops									
riding the horse (crotch torture)									
rituals									
religious scenes									
restrictive rules on behaviour									
rubber/latex clothing									
rope body harness									
scratching (getting)									
scratching (giving)									
sensory deprivation									
serving									
serving as art									
serving as ashtray									
serving as furniture									
serving as maid									
serving as toilet (urine)									
serving as toilet (faeces)									

serving as waitress/ waiter								
serving orally (sexual)								
serving other Dommes/ Doms								
sexual deprivation (short-term)								
sexual deprivation (long-term)								
shaving (body hair)								
shaving (head hair)								
sleep deprivation								
sleep sacks								
slutty clothing (private)								
slutty clothing (public)								
spandex clothing								
spanking								
speech restrictions (when, what)								
speculums (anal)								
speculums (vaginal)								
spreader bars								

APPENDIX A

standing in corner									
stocks									
straight jackets									
strap on dildos (sucking on)									
strap on dildos (penetrated by)									
strap on dildos (wearing)									
strapping (full body beating)									
suspension (upright)									
suspension (inverted)									
suspension (horizontal)									
supplying new partners for Domme/Dom									
swallowing faeces									
swallowing semen									
swallowing urine									
swearing									
swinging (multiple couples)									
tampon training (in arse)									
tattooing									

teasing									
TENS unit (electrical toy)									
thumb cuffs (metal)									
tickling									
triple penetration									
urethral sounds (metal rods)									
uniforms									
vaginal dildo									
verbal humiliation									
vibrator on genitals									
violet wand (electrical toy)									
voyeurism (watching others)									
voyeurism (others watching you)									
voyeurism (your Domme/ Dom & others)									
video (watching others)									
video (recording of you)									
water torture									
waxing (hair removal)									

APPENDIX A

wearing symbolic jewellery								
whipping								
wooden paddles								
wrestling								

*Note: Advise Domme/Dom if you have suffered any of the above and situations that may trigger you during a session.

Appendix B

Sample slavery Agreement

The following pages contain a template of a slavery agreement. Such agreements may be used for a 24/7 full time D/s relationship.

The term of these agreements can run anywhere from three months to several years. This will give both parties a chance to redefine the conditions within the agreement, if necessary.

The sample provided is a good starting point for agreement negotiations. Typically, the Domme/Dom and the sub will verbally state what each of them expects in the proposed 24/7 D/s relationship. The sub should also define any **limits** that will affect the relationship. The agreement template can then be modified by the Domme/Dom to reflect these conditions.

For the purpose of displaying a sample agreement, an imaginary scenario is used where Bob is entering into a twelve-month agreement with his Domme, Mistress Eros. This sample comprises a typical draft of an agreement presented to Bob for his consideration. He would be expected to comment on it. There may be several iterations of this document before both players are satisfied that they have an agreement that is mutually satisfying.

APPENDIX B

slave AGREEMENT FOR slave bob

slave bob (hereafter simply referred to as slave), previously in possession of his own person, agrees and states that he wishes and intends to deliver himself entirely into the hands of Mistress Eros (hereafter reverently referred to as Mistress), his Mistress. Mistress agrees and states that She wishes and intends to take possession of slave.

By signing this slavery agreement, it is agreed that slave gives up all rights to his own person in every manner, and that Mistress takes entire possessions of slave as property, claiming for herself slave's life, slave's future, and slave's heart and mind.

1. slave's Role:

1.1 slave agrees to obey and submit completely to Mistress in all ways. There are no boundaries regarding place, time, or situation in which the slave may wilfully refuse to obey the direction of Mistress.

1.2 slave also agrees that, once entered into the slavery agreement, his body belongs to his Mistress, to be used as seen fit.

1.3 All of slave's possessions likewise belong to Mistress, including all assets, finances, and material goods, to do with as She sees fit.

1.4 slave agrees to please Mistress to the best of his ability, in that he now exists solely for the pleasure of Mistress.

1.5 slave understands that all he has, and all that he does, shall now move from 'right', to 'privilege', granted only as She wishes, and only to the extent that She finds useful.

2. slave's General Behaviour:

2.1 slave will strive diligently to remould slave's body, appearance, habits, and attitudes in accordance with Mistress's desires. slave agrees to change slave's actions, speech, and dress to express the ownership. slave will always speak of his Mistress in terms of love and respect, and will address Her appropriately (i.e. Mistress, Ma'am, etc.) when so directed.

2.2 slave will seek to learn how to please Mistress better and will gracefully accept any criticism in whatever form Mistress chooses.

2.3 slave renounces all rights to privacy or concealment from Mistress. This includes but is not limited to photography and video photography of slave, in any situation, to be used and displayed in any manner Mistress sees fit.

2.4 slave agrees to confess all of slave's desires and fetishes for the Mistress's consideration. slave will answer truthfully and completely, to the best of slave's knowledge, any and all questions Mistress may ask of slave. slave will volunteer any information his Mistress should know about his physical or emotional condition.

2.5 When in the same room as his Mistress, slave will ask permission before leaving the room, explain where he is going, and why. This includes but is not limited to asking permission to use the bathroom.

APPENDIX B

2.6 slave shall be responsible for maintaining the cleanliness and availability of all toys and equipment. None shall be used without the express permission of Mistress, unless agreed to beforehand.

2.7 slave is responsible for maintenance and completion of all household chores. This includes but is not limited to cooking all meals, laundry, cleaning, vacuuming, dusting, maintaining the kitchen and bathrooms, running errands, shopping.

3. slave's Dress/Body/Appearance:

3.1 slave shall diligently maintain and adorn slave's body parts in such a manner as will ensure that they are fully open and available to Mistress. slave's body parts shall be able to be displayed by slave in public or private, to others or to Mistress, when so ordered.

3.2 slave shall never close or cross his legs in Mistress's presence, unless specific permission to do so is granted.

3.3 slave shall never wear undergarments at any time, except when allowed to wear shorts or underpants, and shall cover no part of his body with apparel or material of any description, except when the act of doing so, and the design of the item of apparel or material, are expressly approved by Mistress.

3.4 slave shall keep slave's body parts clean-shaven or waxed at the direction of the Mistress.

3.5 slave shall keep slave's hair cut, styled, and coloured as directed by Mistress.

3.6 Mistress has the right to tattoo or have tattooed, pierce or have pierced, or brand or have branded, slave's body.

3.7 slave will always wear, 24 hours a day, 7 days a week, a token of his possession, given to him by Mistress.

4. Mistress's Role:

Mistress accepts the responsibility of slave's body and worldly possessions, to do with as She sees fit. Mistress agrees to love, care for, protect, and cherish slave, and to arrange for the safety and well-being of slave. Mistress also accepts the commitment to train the slave, punish the slave, love the slave, and use the slave as She sees fit.

5. Punishment:

slave agrees to accept any punishment Mistress decides to inflict, whether earned or not. slave agrees that severe punishment may be assessed for any infraction of the letter or spirit of this slavery agreement and will accept the correction gratefully. The form and extent of the punishment shall be at the Mistress's pleasure. She may punish slave without reason to please Herself. slave enjoys the right to cry, scream, or beg, but accepts the fact that these heartfelt expressions will not affect his treatment. Further, he accepts that if his Mistress tires of his noise, Mistress may gag him or take other actions to silence him.

6. Other People:

6.1 slave may not seek any other Mistress, Master or lover, or relate to others in any sexual or submissive way, either in 'real time', or 'virtual' or 'cyber' space, without Mistress's

APPENDIX B

permission. To do so will be considered a breach of slavery agreement and will result in extreme punishment or slavery agreement termination.

6.2 Mistress may accept other slaves or lovers but must consider slave's emotional response to such actions.

6.3 slave agrees that his Mistress possesses the right to determine whether others can use his body and to what use they may put it. Mistress will discuss all such instances in advance with slave. slave has no say in the choice of these other partners, with the exception that play with others must be 'safe' in terms of the exchange of bodily fluids.

7. Alteration of slavery agreement:

This slavery agreement may not be altered, except when both Mistress and slave agree. If the slavery agreement is altered, the new slavery agreement shall be printed and signed, and then the old slavery agreement must be destroyed.

8. Termination of slavery agreement:

This slavery agreement may be terminated at any time by Mistress, but never by slave. Upon termination, all materials and belongings shall belong to Mistress, to be shared or kept as Mistress sees fit. slave, owning nothing and having agreed to give up all worldly possessions and body to Mistress, shall once again own his body, but nothing else.

Slave's Signature:

I have read and fully understand this slavery agreement in its entirety. I agree to give everything I own to my Mistress, and further accept Her claim of ownership over my physical body, heart, soul, and mind. I understand that I will be commanded and trained and punished as a slave, and I promise to be true and to fulfil the pleasures and desires of my Mistress, and to serve Her to the best of my abilities. I understand that I cannot withdraw from this slavery agreement.

Signature:_____ Date: _____

Witness: _____

Mistress's Signature:

I have read and fully understand this slavery agreement in its entirety. I agree to accept this slave as my property, body and possessions, and to care for him to the best of my ability. I shall provide for him security and wellbeing, and command him, train him, and punish him as a slave. I understand the responsibility implicit in this arrangement and agree that no harm shall come to slave as long as he is mine. I further understand that I can withdraw from this slavery agreement at any time.

Signature:_____ Date: _____

Witness: _____

About the Author

Mistress Flame is a former Dominatrix and is experienced in both sides of the BDSM world, beginning as a submissive and progressing to a Dominant (her preference).

She would use her sub experiences to test new techniques and equipment, giving her an ever-expanding awareness of the topic.

The ability to switch roles and personas make her an excellent transformational coach and author.

She loves to travel and lives in Melbourne with her husband and two cats.

Connect with Mistress Flame on:
www.MistressFlame.com
FB-Domina Flame
Insta-Mistressflame3

ABOUT THE AUTHOR

Birth of a Mistress

Mistress Flame is just completing her next book, Birth of a Mistress, telling the story of a traumatised woman called Elida, entering the world of BDSM. The new world opens up opportunities for her, however it also brings to light her dark and colourful life. Elida's life beginning with childhood abuse and chronic trauma comes back to haunt her as a result of the BDSM world. Follow Elida's journey as she faces and deals with the challenges that are presented to her and the impacts it has on her relationships and her future.

www.ingramcontent.com/pod-product-compliance
Lightning Source LLC
Chambersburg PA
CBHW061245230426
43662CB00020B/2430